John Donne
in the Time of COVID

John Donne
in the Time of COVID

An Analysis of *Devotions upon Emergent Occasions*

MARY ANN ANTLEY

RESOURCE *Publications* • Eugene, Oregon

JOHN DONNE IN THE TIME OF COVID
An Analysis of *Devotions upon Emergent Occasions*

Copyright © 2022 Mary Ann Antley. All rights reserved. Except for brief quotations in critical publications or reviews, no part of this book may be reproduced in any manner without prior written permission from the publisher. Write: Permissions, Wipf and Stock Publishers, 199 W. 8th Ave., Suite 3, Eugene, OR 97401.

Resource Publications
An Imprint of Wipf and Stock Publishers
199 W. 8th Ave., Suite 3
Eugene, OR 97401

www.wipfandstock.com

PAPERBACK ISBN: 978-1-6667-5379-0
HARDCOVER ISBN: 978-1-6667-5380-6
EBOOK ISBN: 978-1-6667-5381-3

11/23/22

To my children, Mills, Catherine, and Angus Antley,
without whom this book would never have been published,
and to my late husband, Dr. Ray M. Antley,
who was supportive of my thought.

Contents

Acknowledgments	ix
Introduction	xi
Prologue: The Illness: Subjectively and Objectively Presented	1
Part I: The Emotional States Experienced by John Donne During Critical Illness and Convalescence	7
Part II: The Structure of the *Devotions*: Adaptation to Change	39
Part III : Psychological, Sociological, Theological, and Psychoanalytical Studies Suggested by the Identification of Donne's Emotional States During Illness	47
A. Stages of Death and Dying, 1623–1973. A Cross-Cultural Study of Kübler-Ross and Donne	48
B. Doctor –Patient Relationship: Threat and Benefit Perception During the Course of a Critical Illness	73
C. Sick Role Adaptive Behavior: Its Relationship to Donne's Emotional Evolution	84
D. Donne's Illness: The Demand for a Redefinition of Ultimacy	88
E. Job and Donne: The Expansion of Awareness through Suffering	92
F. God–Donne Relationship: Crisis Needs—Formula or Process	107
G. John Donne's Life: In Search of Order	127
Epilogue: The Experience: Objectively and Subjectively Perceived	161
"An Elegy Upon the Death of the Dean of Pauls, Dr. John Donne"	164
Appendix 1: Major Poems and Prose	169
Appendix 2: Three Letters from John Donne	171
Appendix 3: John Donne's Mother, Elizabeth Heywood Donne	175

Appendix 4: John Donne's Father, the elder John Donne, Ironmonger 177

Appendix 5: Copernicus and Galileo Galilei 178

Author's Short Bio 179

Bibliography 181

Acknowledgments

The Reverend Alan Koeneke and the Reverend Dr. Marshall Jolly both recognized the importance of this work and encouraged its publication.

Kathy Boozan and Matthew Perreault worked to copyedit it. I appreciate their help and insight.

Introduction

When COVID-19 swept into and through the United States, I immediately thought of John Donne, his illness in 1623, and his record of that illness in *Devotions upon Emergent Occasions* published in 1624. In this work, he describes his emotions from the time he gets sick of a yet unnamed illness until he is well enough for his doctors to dismiss him from their care.

This book is the result of my recognition that Donne describes feelings that are like those identified by Dr. Elizabeth Kübler-Ross in her work with terminally ill patients at the University of Chicago Billings Hospital in mid-twentieth century: anxiety, hostility, depression, hope, and acceptance. Despite a space of nearly four-hundred years, we see that human beings when faced with a major change in their life respond emotionally in a remarkably similar pattern. The following book establishes this fact in its tracing of Donne's illness and his subsequent responses.

Now, however, as we grapple with the spread of a pandemic in the United States and indeed in the entire world, another comparison has emerged—the way our culture is handling the corona virus and the way the plague was approached in the late sixteenth and early seventeenth century in England. The challenges have remained the same: how to respond to a pestilential illness when it emerges; when to mandate isolation; what medicine is effective; what interventions actually help; should a patient be hospitalized; how to cope with burials; how to bring an end to the pandemic itself.

The responses—even after four-hundred years of scientific and medical advances—are again similar: isolation of ill persons, distancing of all persons, wearing special clothing such as masks, gloves, and uniforms as protection from infection, avoidance of large gatherings of persons in churches, schools, sports arenas, and auditoriums. Many persons in both times choose if possible to get out of the city and then shelter at home in a less populated space.

Today, as in the early seventeenth century, when we are isolated from other people, we find ways to pass the time. Donne, as arguably the best prose writer of his time, took notes on his illness from start to finish and went beyond the objective descriptions for the course of the disease found in his meditations to expostulations that related his experience to those persons in scripture who had also gone through a challenging time; and finally, he got closure with a prayer. He chose this medium because preaching, praying, and making relationships between events in this world and the next was what he was called to do as Dean of Saint Paul's Cathedral, and he was the best of his profession. Not many of today's population are as well educated as Donne or have a desire to be a first-rate theologian, but we, too, make connections between what is going on in the world and in our own lives. We relate our feelings in whatever medium our talent lies. And we like Donne, try to survive.

Some behaviors were different in the seventeenth century: doctors made home visits in Donne's time while today they consult via telephone, e-mail and zoom. Donne's consultations with doctors started with his family doctor, who called in other doctors to help diagnose the disease. Finally, the ultimate consult, King James' personal doctor, Sir Théodore de Mayerne, paid a visit. We aren't told if it is he who helps make the diagnosis, but Donne seems in better spirits for the attention given him.

After the disease has a name, the doctors set out to treat with medicines and procedures. Donne is given cordials to drink. He is given a poultice made of pigeons to be placed on his feet to draw the fever out of his head; then he is purged. He survives both medicine and treatments and is declared on the way to recovery. This doesn't happen at once. He is too weak to stand up. But he lives and is determined to share his experience with others. *Devotions upon Emergent Occasions* was published several months later and went through five editions in the seventeenth century. It is there for us, today.

> No man is an *Iland*, intire of it selfe; every man is a peece of the *Continent*, a part of the *maine*; if a *Clod* bee washed away by the *Sea, Europe* is the lesse, as well as if a *Promontorie* were, as well as if a *Mannor* of thy *friends* or of *thine owne* were; any mans *death* diminishes *me*, because I am involved in *Mankinde*; And therefore never send to know for whom the *bell* tolls; It tolls for *thee*.
> —Meditation XVII, *Devotions upon Emergent Occasions*
>   John Donne, 1623

Prologue

The Illness: Subjectively and Objectively Presented

Thou hast made me, And shall thy worke decay?
Repaire me now, for now mine end doth haste,
I runne to death, and death meets me as fast,
And all my pleasures are like yesterday;
I dare not move my dimme eyes any way,
Despaire behind, and death before doth cast
Such terrour, and my feeble flesh doth waste
By sinne in it, which it t'wards hell doth weigh;
Onely thou art above, and when towards thee
By thy leave I can looke, I rise againe;
But our old subtle foe so tempteth me,
That not one houre my selfe I can sustaine;
Thy Grace may wing me to prevent his art,
And thou like Adamant draw mine iron heart.
—*Holy Sonnet I*, John Donne[1]

---

1. Grierson, *Metaphysical*, 85.

The Illness: Donne's Description

In the latter part of November 1623, John Donne was suddenly taken ill with a fever. He describes the physical illness itself in his *Devotions upon Emergent Occasions*:

Variable, and therfore miserable condition of Man; this minute I was well, and am ill, this minute. I am surpriz'd with a sodaine change, and alteration to worse, and can impute it to no cause, nor call it by any name. We study *Health*, and we deliberate upon our *meats*, and *drink*, and *ayre*, and *exercises*, and we hew, and wee polish every stone, that goes to that building; and so our *Health* is a long and a regular work; But in a minute a Canon batters all, overthrowes all, demolishes all; a *Sicknes* unprevented for all our diligence, unsuspected for all our curiositie; nay, undeserved, if we consider only *disorder*, summons us, seizes us, possesses us, destroyes us in an instant.[2]

He continues—"in the same instant that I feele the first attempt of the disease, I feele the victory; In the twinckling of an eye, I can scarse see, instantly the tast is insipid, and fatuous; instantly the appetite is dull and desirelesse: instantly the knees are sinking and strengthlesse; and in an instant, sleepe . . . is taken away. . . . I sweat againe, and againe, from the brow, to the sole of the foot, but I eat no bread, I tast no sustenance."[3]

He subsequently goes to bed, is visited by his doctor, by other consulting physicians, and finally by the king's physician. Medicine is prescribed, but despite its administration, the disease is not arrested. "My forces are not enfeebled, I find no decay in my strength; my provisions are not cut off, I find no abhorring in mine appetite; my counsels are not corrupted or infatuated, I find no false apprehensions, to work upon mine understanding; and yet . . . I feele, that insensibly the *disease* prevailes."[4] In response to this advancement, Donne is given cordials "to keep the venim and Malignitie of the disease from the Heart," and has pidgeons applied to his feet "to draw the vapors from the Head."[5] Finally, "the Sicknes declares the infection and malignity thereof by spots;" . . . however, "if there be a *comfort* in the declaration, that therby the *Phisicians* see more cleerely what to doe, there may bee as much *discomfort* in this, That the malignitie may bee so great, as that all that they can doe, shall doe *nothing*."[6] The doctors now tell him that

---

2. Donne, *Devotions* (Sparrow), 1.
3. Donne, *Devotions* (Sparrow), 6–7.
4. Donne, *Devotions* (Sparrow), 56.
5. Donne, *Devotions* (Sparrow), 60; Donne, *Devotions* (Sparrow), 67.
6. Donne, *Devotions* (Sparrow), 74.

his illness has reached the critical days. Donne cannot sleep and asks "why, since I have lost my delight in all objects, cannot I discontinue the facultie of seeing them, by closing mine *eies* in *sleepe*?"[7] He lies awake, listening to the passing bell tolling for another man's dying, aware that he, himself, is near death. But the crisis passes; Donne does not die; and with the aid of his physicians, who purge him, he begins the long process of recuperation. His weakness—"I cannot *rise* out of my bed, till the *Physitian enable* mee, nay I cannot tel, that I am able to rise, till *hee tell* me so"—is even more apparent when he tries to stand up.[8] "I am readier to fall to the *Earth*, now I am up, than I was when I *lay* in the bed . . . I am *up*, and I seeme to *stand*, and I goe *round* . . . for a long time I was not able to *rise*; At last, I must bee *raised* by others; and now I am *up*, I am ready to sinke *lower* than before."[9] Once again, he is purged to eradicate the disease and finally, at the end of his illness, he is warned to take care of himself to avoid a relapse. He remains weak for a long time. "Though I have left my bed, I have not left my bedside. I sit there still, and as a Prisoner discharged, sits at the Prison doore, to beg Fees, So sit I here."[10]

It was during this period of convalescence that Donne organized the notes taken while he was ill into the *Devotions upon Emergent Occasions*. "I am . . . in a convalescence, when I thought my self varie near my period. God brought me into a low valley, and from thence shewed me high Jerusalem, upon so high a hill, as that he thought it fit to bid me stay, and gather more breath. This I do, by meditating, by expostulating, by praying; for, since I am barred of my ordinarie diet, which is Reading, I make these my exercises, which is another part of Physick."[11]

The Illness: Clinical Description

From this detailed account of Donne's physical illness, a medical diagnosis of relapsing fever has been suggested.[12] The following clinical description of this disease is taken from Cecil and Loeb's *Textbook of Medicine*:

> The initial attack may last two to seven or more days. It usually starts abruptly with chilliness or a chill followed by a high

---

7. Donne, *Devotions* (Sparrow), 88.
8. Donne, *Devotions* (Sparrow), 127.
9. Donne, *Devotions* (Sparrow), 127–28.
10. Coffin, *Complete Poetry*, 395.
11. Coffin, *Complete Poetry*, 395–6.
12. Shapiro, "Walton," 20–21.

fever, intense headache, pains in the muscles and joints, nausea, vomiting, photophobia, dizziness and sometimes epistaxis. The temperature rises quickly to 104° or 105° or higher, and except for slight morning remissions it remains elevated throughout the initial febrile period, at the end of which it falls to normal by crisis. The pulse also rises quickly and soon reaches 110 to 140 beats per minute. Periods of sweating may occur during the first day, thereafter the skin is hot and dry, and the face is flushed. Jaundice may occur, but is more likely to appear later. An erythematous rash is common during this period, and later rose–coloreds spots may occur on the trunk and limbs.

Frequently the patient complains of severe headaches and of muscular and joint pains. In case of high fever there may be delirium. Insomnia may be an important symptom, and hyperesthesias of the taste and tactile senese may occur... The period of the initial attack usually ends abruptly with profuse sweating and a rapid fall of the temperature to normal or below. This may be accompanied by diarrhea. In elderly or weak patients, a dangerous state of collapse may occur.

The first period of apyrexia which follows the crisis of the initial attack lasts three to ten days. The fever and all other symptoms subside. The spirochetes disappear from the peripheral blood stream. The skin becomes cool and pale, and the pulse falls to the normal rate and is of poor quality. The prostration is great at first, but in a few days the appetite and strength return and the patient feels so well that he considers himself completely recovered.

The first relapse follows this symptomless interval. It is characterized by a repetition of the more important symptoms of the initial attack. It may be more severe, but, as a rule, it is milder... The relapse seldom lasts as long as the first attack, and it also ends by crisis.

Subsequent Relapses: The end of the first relapse is often coincident with convalescence, but in many instances additional relapses occur. Frequently these are shorter and milder than the previous febrile periods. Convalescence may be protracted.[13]

Although a comparison of the medical description of relapsing fever to Donne's description of his illness attests to his abilities of accurate scientific observation, his *Devotions upon Emergent Occasions* is not primarily concerned with the clinical course of the disease. Rather, the poet overtly uses the illness as the basis for a series of twenty–three devotional exercises,

---

13. Cecil and Loeb, *Textbook of Medicine*, 380–85.

each divided into three parts of meditation, expostulation, and prayer, in which various philosophical and theological problems are related to stages of the illness and analyzed within this framework.

It is in the context of devotional literature that this book has formerly been reviewed. If, however, the work is read with specific attention focused on the dynamics of Donne's psychological responses to a serious illness, it may be seen to be the powerful dramatic presentation of the man's struggle for emotional and spiritual survival following the disruption of a previously accepted value system. It is the purpose of this book to identify the psychological responses to illness which are revealed in the *Devotions upon Emergent Occasions*, to trace the progression of these responses, and to discuss the significance of the total experience that is revealed from a psychological, a sociological, a theological, and a psychoanalytical viewpoint.

Part I

The Emotional States Experienced by John Donne During A Critical Illness and Convalescence

Death, be not proud, though some have called thee
Mighty and dreadfull, for, thou art not soe,
For, those, whom thou think'st thou dost overthrow,
Die not, poore death, nor yet canst thou kill mee.
From rest and sleepe, which but thy pictures bee,
Much pleasure, then from thee, much more must flow,
And soonest our best men with thee doe goe,
Rest of their bones, and soules deliverie.
Thou art slave to Fate, Chance, kings, and desperate men,
And dost with poyson, warre, and sicknesse dwell,
And poppie or charmes can make us sleepe as well,
And better than thy stroake; why swell'st thou then?
One short sleepe past, wee wake eternally,
And death shall be no more; death, thou shalt die.
—*Holy Sonnet X*: John Donne[1]

---

1. Grierson, *Metaphysical*, 87.

Devotions upon Emergent Occasions presents a record of John Donne's emotional responses throughout a critical illness. The frustration caused by the disruption of normal patterns of life that occurs during illness, the impotency felt when placed in a totally dependent position with the stakes as high as life itself, and the loneliness attendant upon the physical and mental isolation of the sick which separates them from meaningful communication with other men, are followed by fear, aroused over the possible course and outcome of the illness, and depression, which comes when coping mechanisms are no longer able to ward off hard contemplation of man's frailty and his ultimate inability to control his fate.

It is only after these emotional states have been intensely experienced that Donne is able to reach an acceptance of his situation. The dependency of illness has reaffirmed that ground of interdependency that underlies each life. It is a human thing to need and accept aid, as well as to give it. It is human to suffer and to die, and there is corporateness in this seemingly unique individual experience. "No man is an *Iland*, intire of it selfe; every man is a peece of the *Continent*, a part of the *maine*; if a *Clod* bee washed away by the *Sea*, Europe is the lesse, as well as if a *Promontorie* were, as well as if a *Mannor* of thy *friends* or of *thine owne* were; any mans *death* diminishes *me*, because I am involved in *Mankinde*."[2] Following this acceptance, Donne experiences positive feelings about his situation. The doctor is doing a good job, the medicines that he uses are effective; Donne, himself, has the will to fight, and he hopes for a recovery. And finally, when indeed it appears that the illness is subsiding, and that convalescence will eventually give way to normal health, it is with some anxiety that Donne readjusts to caring for himself once more.

Thus Donne, during the course of an illness, experiences the emotions of anger, loneliness, fear, depression, acceptance, and hope. These stages correspond to the psychological states that Dr. Elizabeth Kübler-Ross observed in dying patients.[3] Furthermore, they illustrate various stages which occur in the process of adaptation to sick–role behavior. Finally, these emotional states may be seen as stages in a spiritual identity crisis that arises when sudden and severe illness makes Donne aware of his vulnerability as a human being—a crisis which is resolved when he is able to accept his humanity and his place in the universe. It is, of course, recognized that these three processes—the psychological, sociological, and spiritual—do not function independently of each other, and are indeed, interdependent in their dynamics and expression. However, for the purpose of analyzation, they will

---

2. Donne, *Devotions* (Sparrow), 98.
3. Kübler-Ross, *On Death and Dying*, 51–156.

be studied separately, in order that the specific insights that are gained from each model may be explored fully within that framework.

It is also apparent that this is a study of a particular illness, relapsing fever, and its emotional effect on a particular person, John Donne. The circumstances of that illness, the coping mechanisms, even the method chosen to record the illness, are all directly related to the time and place in which Donne lived—late sixteenth and early seventeenth century England—and to the circumstances of Donne's own life. The fact that he was raised a Roman Catholic in a time of Roman Catholic persecution, that he was a scholar in a time of secular and theological change, a one-time courtier, an Anglican convert risen to the Deanship of St. Paul's Cathedral, and a recognized writer of poetry and prose all influence the structure and content of this work. The distance of nearly 400 years not only affords the opportunity for a holistic view of the age and the man, but also extends the meaning of the psychological and sociological phenomena associated with sickness and dying which are being studied by social scientists today.

We have, then, a study in the psychology of the dying patient, in sick role adaptation, and in spiritual conflict that is based not on generalizations arrived at from studying many subjects, but rather from the in-depth probing into a very detailed account of one such experience. Having established that Donne does experience certain feelings, the work offers significant insight into the utilization of coping mechanisms, and may be analyzed for that alone. This multifaceted interpretation of Donne's illness will also, it is hoped, add insight into the complex personality of John Donne and may in turn, be helpful for those scholars who analyze his writing. Finally, it is anticipated that the following analysis will be useful not only to the various specialists, but to the general reading public as well; for the work, whose subject is universally applicable when read in its totality, offers a catharsis that is unique in Donne's own writing and that places it in the great tradition of English dramatic literature. The impact, which was recognized in its own time and which caused it to have five editions within twenty years of its first publication, is still present today.[4] We *are* Donne—insecure in a world of rapid philosophical and scientific change; unable to control this world and seeking for stability in a microcosm of our own design which is also ultimately subject to the effect of change. We, as he, must cope with the trauma of surviving when basic values are threatened, and when external circumstances force an adjustment of behavior. And we, too, fight back by incorporating our life's experiences into our crisis coping mechanisms.

---

4. Donne, *Devotions* (Sparrow), vii.

Identification of Emotional States

Anger

"Variable, and therfore miserable condition of Man; this minute I was well, and am ill, this minute. I am surpriz'd with a sodaine change, and alteration to worse, and can impute it to no cause, nor call it by any name."[5] Thus, Donne begins his account of his illness by describing its onset. It is sudden, of unknown etiology and origin, unexpected, unidentified, and painful, and Donne's initial response is one of diffuse anger. Anger at the disruption of his life, the immediate loss of health, the physical discomfort, and the anxiety that he feels in relationship to these occurrences, an anxiety which he sees to be harmful to his prognosis, yet he is unable to control. From the very beginning, then, there is a recognition of the effect of his emotions on his illness and of the fact that there is both an emotional and a physical response to illness, neither of which is within his control and both of which are painful to experience.

After this initial outpouring of diffuse distress at this illness, Donne devotes an entire meditation to the description of the physical symptoms of his illness: "In the same instant that I feele the first attempt of the disease, I feele the victory; In the twinckling of an eye, I can scarse see, instantly the tast is insipid, and fatuous; instantly the appetite is dull and desirelesse: instantly the knees are sinking and strengthlesse; and in an instant, sleepe, which is the *picture*, the *copie* of *death*, is taken away, that the *Originall*, *Death* it selfe may succeed, and that so I might have death to the life . . . I sweat againe, and againe, from the brow, to the sole of the foot, but I eat no bread, I tast no sustenance."[6]

This devastating illness, which has altered his health, also calls for alteration in his lifestyle. He is confined to bed, is dependent upon the aid of a doctor and, except for the doctor, is isolated from contact with other people. The primary emotional response to this period of adjustment is that of anger. An entire meditation is spent in an outcry against being bedridden. It is inhuman to have to lie prone. "Wee attribute but one priviledge and advantage to Mans body, above other moving creatures, that he is not as others, groveling, but of an erect, of an upright form, naturally built, and disposed to the contemplation of *Heaven*."[7] It is preparation for death. "When *God* came to breath into *Man* the breath of life, he found him flat upon the ground; when he comes to withdraw that breath from him againe,

---

5. Donne, *Devotions* (Sparrow), 1.
6. Donne, *Devotions* (Sparrow), 6–7.
7. Donne, *Devotions* (Sparrow), 10.

hee prepares him to it, by laying him flat upon his bed."[8] To lie in bed is worse than being in prison for "Scarse any prison so close, that affords not the prisoner two, or three steps."[9] It is more restrictive than "the *Anchorites* that barqu'd themselves up in hollowe trees," or than a man that "barrell'd himselfe in a Tubb" because it allows no change in position.[10] A sick bed is, in fact, a grave and to be in a sick bed is worse than to be in your grave because in your grave you may instruct your friends thru your epitaph, whereas you scare them and cause them anxiety when you lie sick.[11] In this passage, Donne's resistance to being bedridden comes out in the imagery, and the extent of treatment of the subject. As in so many other parts of the *Devotions*, the suddenness and severity of the illness, which offers him no choice of a gradual adaptation to sick role behavior, accentuate his adjustment problem and result in a strongly expressed frustration.

This frustration is expressed in the following meditation also, in which Donne contemplates another aspect of being ill—the dependency upon a doctor for recovery. This is a second area in which his illness demands an adjustment in behavior. He must give up his responsibility for his own health to another person. Just as going to bed becomes symbolic of a loss of independence of action, calling a doctor becomes symbolic for loss of self-sufficiency:

> We *have* the *Phisician*, but we *are not* the *Phisician*. Heere we shrinke in our proportion, sink in our dignitie, in respect of verie meane creatures, who are *Phisicians* to themselves. The *Hart* that is pursued and wounded, they say, knowes an Herbe, which being eaten, throwes off the arrow: A strange kind of *vomit*. . . Man hath not that *innate instinct*, to apply these naturall medicines to his present danger, as those inferiour creatures have; he is not his owne *Apothecary*, his owne *Phisician*, as they are. . . His *diseases* are his owne, but the *Phisician* is not; hee hath them at home, but hee must send for the *Phisician*.[12]

---

8. Donne, *Devotions* (Sparrow), 10.
9. Donne, *Devotions* (Sparrow), 10.
10. Donne, *Devotions* (Sparrow), 10–11.
11. Donne, *Devotions* (Sparrow), 11.
12. Donne, *Devotions* (Sparrow), 17.

Loneliness

Finally, in this period of adjustment to the conditions placed upon him by illness, there is the meditation devoted to loneliness. Relapsing fever was a communicable disease similar in many ways to plague, and Donne is literally deserted by his friends.[13] His primary contact with people is the physician, who, despite the fact that he is a friend, is a reminder of Donne's own inability to care for himself and on whom, as will be shown later, Donne focuses his anxiety over the outcome of the disease.

"The Phisician comes. Solus adest (He only)." These are the English and the Latin headings for the meditation, which leaves the doctor to consider the acute loneliness of the sick. Again, the type of illness and the rapid onset heighten the problem, the abrupt change accentuates the contrast of his normal social behavior, in which as Dean of St. Paul's he must have had a full and demanding life, to his sick room solitude.

There remains a universality in this passage that is equally applicable today. "As *Sicknes* is the greatest misery, so the greatest misery of sicknes, is *solitude*; when the infectiousnes of the disease deterrs them who should assist, from comming; even the *Phisician* dares scarse come. *Solitude* is a torment which is not threatened in *hell* it selfe."[14] He recognizes the reasons that he is not visited. "When I am but sick, and might infect, they have no remedy, but their absence, and my solitude. It is an *excuse* to them that are *great*, and pretend, and yet are loth to come; it is an *inhibition* to those who would truly come, because they may be made instruments and pestiducts, to the infection of others, by their comming."[15] Thus, "a long sicknesse will weary friends at last, but a pestientiall sicknes averts them from the beginning."[16] He further elaborates that "it is an *Outlawry*, an *Excommunication* upon the *Patient*, and seperats him from all offices not onely of *Civilitie*, but of *working Charitie*."[17] This separation, this loneliness, Donne sees as aberrant from both heavenly and earthly norms. "*God* himself wold admit a *figure* of *Society*, as there is a plurality of persons in *God*, though there bee but one *God*; and all his externall actions testifie a love of *Societie*, and *communion*."[18] And "*God*, who sawe that all that hee made, was good, came not so neer seeing a *defect* in any of his works, as when he saw that

---

13. Bald, *Donne*, 454.
14. Donne, *Devotions* (Sparrow), 22.
15. Donne, *Devotions* (Sparrow), 22.
16. Donne, *Devotions* (Sparrow), 23.
17. Donne, *Devotions* (Sparrow), 22–23.
18. Donne, *Devotions* (Sparrow), 23.

it was not good, for man to bee *alone*, therefore *hee made him a helper*; and one that should help him so, as to increase the *number*, and give him her owne and *more societie*."[19] Just as being bedridden is seen as worse than being in a grave, an infectious bed is also compared with burial. "Thogh in both I be equally alone, in my bed I *know* it, and *feele* it, and shall not in my *grave*: and this too, that in my bedd, my soule is still in an infectious body, and shall not in my grave bee so."[20]

There is less anger in this meditation. The stark statement of the situation and the feelings this causes have none of the resentment that comes out in the treatment of being bedridden and of dependency on the doctor. Perhaps this is because these former passages are concerned with the imposed dependency of the sick in which Donne is literally acknowledging his impotency by outward behavior. Loneliness, while different from normal behavior, and seen by Donne as unnatural, does not involve this enforced dependency.

Fear

Following the introduction and the four meditations on the physical symptoms, confinement in bed, dependency on the doctor, and loneliness—which may be grouped under the heading of sick role adaptive behavior, and which elicit feelings of anger from Donne—there seems to be less concern with the physical changes in lifestyle that are required of the patient and a mounting concern with the course of the illness itself.

The two pairs of meditations which make up this stage are separated by a passage in which Donne thinks of the quality of wellness—a section which contrasts with his own increasingly precarious situation. The structure for these meditations is also different from the earlier sections. In the earlier group, Donne takes a characteristic and protests against it. In these passages, however, he observes the physician and reacts to his behavior as a means of focusing on and expressing his own fear and, finally, after defining his anxiety, he uses various coping mechanisms as aids in handling this fear.

The Sixth Meditation, for example, centers around the doctor's attempt to disguise his concern and the reaction that Donne has to this dissembling. Donne "observe[s] the *Phisician*, with the same diligence, as hee the *disease*; I see hee *feares*, and I feare with him: I overtake him, I overrun him in his feare, and I go the faster, because he makes his pace slow; I feare the more, because he disguises his fear, and I see it with the more sharpnesse, because

19. Donne, *Devotions* (Sparrow), 23.
20. Donne, *Devotions* (Sparrow), 24.

hee would not have me see it. He knowes that his *feare* shall not disorder the practise, and exercise of his *Art*, but he knows that my *fear* may disorder the effect, and working of his practise."[21] No *explication de texte* is necessary for this keen observation. The new emotion that is introduced here is fear. "Metuit" (I fear) "The Phisician is afraid."[22] Donne's anxiety over the possible outcome of the disease, the subject for these four meditations, is focused in the sixth meditation on the doctor's ill-disguised concern. He follows the initial statement of the situation with several coping mechanisms. First, there is the digression on the various ways fear may manifest itself. "As the *wind* in the body will counterfet any disease, and seem the *stone,* and seem the *Gout,* so *feare* will counterfet any disease of the *Mind*."[23] This is followed by examples: "It shall seeme *love,* a love of having, and it is but a *fear,* a jealous, and suspitious feare of loosing," and he continues on to consider other seemingly inconsistent fears that people have.[24] After this analytical tour de force, Donne returns to the present situation and advances the argument. "I know not, what fear is, nor I know not what it is that I fear now," following it immediately with another flood of examples that help him cope with his problem.[25] "I feare not the hastening of my *death,* and yet I do fear the increase of the *disease*; I should belie *Nature*, if I should deny that I feared this, and if I should say that I feared *death*, I should belye *God*."[26] Whether these assertions are an accurate appraisal of Donne's fears, or statements about what he will allow himself to feel, or even a stated defense against those fears which he knows he has—no matter how incongruous they are from his theological and philosophical position—it is sufficient here to say that they are used to manage his great anxiety and that these definitions are his way of localizing and then controlling his distress. The comparison with which he closes the meditation continues to serve this coping function by offering some closure on the previous discussion. "As my *Phisicians* fear puts not him from his *practise,* neither doth mine put me, from receiving from *God,* and *Man,* and *my selfe, spirituall,* and *civill,* and *morall* assistances, and consolations."[27] Once again, although this is a positive statement, it also contains an element of hope that this is true and continues to suggest the cause for Donne's anxiety about the physician—i.e. the doctor's ability to

21. Donne, *Devotions* (Sparrow), 28.
22. Donne, *Devotions* (Sparrow), 28.
23. Donne, *Devotions* (Sparrow), 28.
24. Donne, *Devotions* (Sparrow), 28.
25. Donne, *Devotions* (Sparrow), 28.
26. Donne, *Devotions* (Sparrow), 28–29.
27. Donne, *Devotions* (Sparrow), 29.

deliver good medical care, as well as about himself, that his illness may alter his relationship with God, man, and himself.

The second meditation in this group continues the initial pattern: a statement of the problem, a specific example of this problem which is followed by a discussion filled with analysis that serves to aid in handling his anxiety, and finally, some closure of the problem. Fear is the primary concern again. "There is *more feare*, therefore *more cause*."[28] It is a dual fear again. First, in concern over establishing the correct diagnosis, the doctor has decided to ask for consults; and second, Donne is concerned over the necessity to have additional doctors. He sees that "the Phisician desires to have others joyned with him," and interprets this to mean "if the *Phisician* desire help, the burden grows great: There is a growth of the *Disease* then."[29] That, of course, is Donne's concern—that consultation equals advance of illness. But instead of continuing to elaborate on his anxiety, he stops, goes back to the problem that aroused it—i.e. the consultation, and enumerates all the positive meanings of the consultation. First of all, the doctor's willingness to have consults is an indication that he is a good physician because "his desiring of others, argues his *candor*, and his *ingenuitie*; if the danger be *great*, he *justifies* his proceedings, and he *disguises* nothing, that calls in *witnesses*; And if the danger bee not *great*, hee is not *ambitious*, that is so readie to divide the thankes, and the honour of that work, which he begun alone, with others."[30] Not only is consultation the sign of a good physician, he continues, the diagnosis is apt to be better when it is shared. "The danger is not the more, and the providence is the more, wher there are more *Phisicians*; as the State is the happier, where businesses are carried by more counsels, than can bee in one breast, how large soever."[31] From these two observations on the advantages of consultation, Donne then goes on to less pertinent and less relevant analogies. Diseases consult how they may win, so why shouldn't doctors? Men may expect death when they are old, but during youth, death is a surprise that may take many forms "and we need so many *Phisicians*, as may make up a *Watch*, and spie every inconvenience."[32] Then follows a list of unexpected ways one may die, with Donne finally bringing back his digression "And therfore the more assistants, the better; who comes to a day of hearing, in a cause of any importance, with one *Advocate*?"[33]

28. Donne, *Devotions* (Sparrow), 35.
29. Donne, *Devotions* (Sparrow), 35.
30. Donne, *Devotions* (Sparrow), 35.
31. Donne, *Devotions* (Sparrow), 35.
32. Donne, *Devotions* (Sparrow), 35.
33. Donne, *Devotions* (Sparrow), 36.

With this in mind, Donne concludes that "as long as we can, let us admit as much *helpe* as wee can; Another, and another *Phisician*, is not another, and another *Indication*, and *Symptom* of death, but another, and another *Assistant*, and *Proctor* of *life*: Nor doe they so much feed the imagination with apprehension of *danger*, as the understanding with *comfort*."[34]

Having temporarily exhausted the subject of the advantages of multiple aid, Donne now shifts to an enumeration of reasons why he should be thankful for his situation. This digression cites examples of those less fortunate who lie ill at home without any doctor, or who may not have a home at all and are "thrown into *Hospitals*, where, (as a fish left upon the Sand, must stay the tide) they must stay the *Phisicians* houre of visiting, and then can bee but *visited*?"[35] Or even worse, those who "have not this *Hospitall* to cover them ... but have their *Grave–stone* under them, and breathe out the soules in the eares, and in the eies of passengers, harder than their bed, the flint of the street."[36] The passage closes with a prayer which offers closure. "O my *soule*, when thou art not enough awake, to blesse thy *God* enough for his plentifull mercy, in affoording thee many *Helpers*, remember how many lacke them, and helpe them to them, or to those other things, which they lacke as much as them."[37] This digression, while filled with accurate observations, is not pertinent to the central problem of Donne's fear over the increase of his illness. Instead, it shows how he has changed the emphasis from his deteriorating condition, as symbolized by the doctors, to a concern over his need to justify the doctors when so many people need them and did not have their aid.

The entire passage shows Donne's fear and the skillful mechanisms he uses in handling that fear. In both of these meditations, Donne has transferred his fear onto the Doctor and discussed it one step removed from himself. This technique is in itself a very effective coping device. Other devices include "talking the problem out," exploring the situation's implications logically rather than emotionally, making analogies to other areas, and comparing his life with those less fortunate.

Following these two sections in which Donne works with his feelings of fear, there is a meditation that explores the resemblance of a king to God. Its conclusion, however, contains a strong positive statement about appreciating and experiencing good health: "No man is well, that understands not, that values not his being well; that hath not a cheerefulnesse, and a joy in

---

34. Donne, *Devotions* (Sparrow), 36.
35. Donne, *Devotions* (Sparrow), 37.
36. Donne, *Devotions* (Sparrow), 37.
37. Donne, *Devotions* (Sparrow), 37.

it; and whosoever hath this *Joy*, hath a desire to communicate, to propagate that, which occasions his happinesse, and his *Joy*, to others; for every man loves witnesses of his happinesse; and the best witnesses, are experimentall witnesses; they who have tasted of that in themselves, which makes us happie."[38] Health then, is not simply freedom from disease, but a positive appreciation of wellbeing, which, when experienced in oneself, causes one to wish to share the experience with others who have also known this feeling. It is a statement of an appreciation for the fullness of life in the midst of a crisis that has both physically and psychologically limited Donne's ability to participate in health. His anxiety over himself and his consuming personal fears restrict his capacity to care for others, just as the severity of his disease restricts his ability to continue normal social interaction. The juxtaposition of true well behavior here offers relief from Donne's abnormal state and serves as a norm with which to compare his subsequent behavior.

Following this interlude, Donne resumes his anxious exploration of the doctor's actions. The action under scrutiny this time is the manner in which they consult and prescribe. "They have seene me, and heard mee, arraign'd mee in these fetters, and receiv'd the *evidence*; I have cut up mine *Anatomy*, dissected my selfe, and they are gon to *read* upon me."[39] He is fearful over this consultation. "O how manifold, and perplexed a thing, nay, how wanton and various a thing is *ruine* and *destruction*?"[40] There are not even names enough for all the illnesses suffered by man, he observes, and even when illness is limited to encompass only fevers, "it would overlode, and oppress any naturall, disorder and discompose any artificiall *Memory*, to deliver the *names* of severall *fevers* . . . and then what it would do, and then how it may be countermind."[41] This awareness of the difficulty of establishing a diagnosis and the possibility for error causes Donne to lack the confidence in the physician that might exist if he were less knowledgeable. His concern is again expressed in terms of worrying over the doctor's actions, rather than in the first person. This anxiety is coped with by the argument that he is glad they have time to consult, which he takes as a sign that his illness is not so desperate as to call for immediate action. "But even in *ill*, it is a degree of *good*, when the *evil* wil admit *consultation*."[42] In the examples that he gives to develop this thesis, Donne's acute observation of human behavior is apparent: "In many *diseases*, that which is but an

38. Donne, *Devotions* (Sparrow), 43.
39. Donne, *Devotions* (Sparrow), 48.
40. Donne, *Devotions* (Sparrow), 48.
41. Donne, *Devotions* (Sparrow), 49.
42. Donne, *Devotions* (Sparrow), 49.

accident, but a *symptom* of the main *disease*, is so violent, that the *Phisician* must attend the cure of that, though hee pretermit (so far as to intermit) the cure of the *disease* it self . . . If a *cholerick* man be ready to strike, must I goe about to purge his *choler*, or to breake the blow? But where there is room for *consultation*, things are not desperate."[43]

From these objective examples, he suddenly becomes personal again, going over to himself the behavior of his physicians. "They *consult*; so there is nothing *rashly, inconsideratly* done; and then they *prescribe*, they *write*, so there is nothing *covertly, disguisedly, unavowedly* done."[44] This is once more followed by objective examples: "In *bodily diseases* it is not alwaies so; sometimes, as soon as the *Phisicians* foote is in the *chamber*, his *knife* is in the patients *arme*; the disease would not allow a *minutes* forbearing of *blood*, nor *prescribing* of other remedies. In States and matter of government it is so too; they are somtimes surprizd with such *accidents*, as that the *Magistrat* asks not what may be done by *law*, but does that, which must necessarily be don in that case."[45] Then comes, for the third time, Donne's recurring concern over the course of treatment. "They who have received my *Anatomy* of my selfe, *consult*, and end their *consultation* in *prescribing*, and in prescribing *Phisick*; proper and convenient remedy."[46] He now reassures himself that this is the correct procedure, with the argument that obviously the doctors are doing the correct thing to treat the illness he has, rather than to tell him what he should have done to stay well, or to tell him how to behave if he gets well.

Again, the examples, and then the closure—which reiterates now for the *fourth* time the doctor's behavior and an avowed approval of this course. "I am glad they know (I have hid nothing from them) glad they consult, (they hide nothing from one another) glad they write (they hide nothing from the world) glad that they write and prescribe *Phisick*, that there are *remedies* for the present case."[47] This closure, following such a careful examination of the physicians, seems shaky despite its assertiveness. It is a resolution of the mind rather than the emotions as Donne, learned in his own right about medicinal techniques,[48] struggles to accept the judgment of his doctors. He checks their behavior, step by step, analyzes and reanalyzes their moves, fearing the possible mistakes and the effect that those would have on his own life struggle.

43. Donne, *Devotions* (Sparrow), 49.
44. Donne, *Devotions* (Sparrow), 49.
45. Donne, *Devotions* (Sparrow), 49–50.
46. Donne, *Devotions* (Sparrow), 50.
47. Donne, *Devotions* (Sparrow), 50.
48. Allen, "Renaissance Medicine," 322–42.

In the last meditation in this group, Meditation X, Donne's fears over the abilities of his doctors seem to be borne out. The physick has not worked as the heading—again in objective terms of the physician—announces: "They find the Disease to steale on insensibly, and endeavour to meet with it so."[49] Just as in the previous meditation, he begins his contemplation in a low vein. Previously, he noted the difficulty of arriving at a diagnosis; now he observes how all things save the light of God, are eventually drawn toward ruin. Men's lives, national states, even the world itself, must face ultimate annihilation.

Having established this somber tone, he moves on to examine the ways this destruction may occur. Sometimes it may be expected and prepared for; other times it's coming is unknown and unexpected. The examples used here are the coming of the zodiac Dog Star, which can be anticipated, as compared with the occurrence of a comet or a blazing star which is apart from the natural understood order of the heavens. The conclusion here is "that which is most *secret*, is most *dangerous*."[50] This is followed by three examples concerned with survival. "Twentie *rebellious drums* make not so dangerous a noise, as a few *whisperers*, and secret plotters in corners. The *Canon* doth not so much hurt against a wal, as a *Myne* under the wall; nor a thousand enemies that threaten, so much as a few that take an *oath* to say *nothing*."[51] The fourth example places a biblical judgment against such covert behavior. "*God* knew many heavy sins of the people, in the wildernes and after, but still he charges them with that one, with *Murmuring, murmuring* in their *hearts*, secret disobediences, secret repugnances against his declar'd wil; and these are the most deadly, the most pernicious."[52] Then swiftly, Donne links his examples with his condition and we are back with him in his bedchamber, fighting off anxieties over the advancing illness:

> And it is so to, with the *diseases* of the *body*; and that is my case. The *pulse*, the *urine*, the *sweat*, all have sworn to say nothing, to give no *Indication*, of any dangerous *sicknesse*. My forces are not enfeebled, I find no decay in my strength; my provisions are not cut off, I find no abhorring in mine appetite; my counsels are not corrupted or infatuated, I find no false apprehensions, to work upon mine understanding; and yet they see, that invisibly, and I feele, that insensibly the *disease* prevailes. The *disease* hath established a *Kingdome*, an *Empire* in mee, and will have certaine

49. Donne, *Devotions* (Sparrow), 54.
50. Donne, *Devotions* (Sparrow), 55.
51. Donne, *Devotions* (Sparrow), 55.
52. Donne, *Devotions* (Sparrow), 55–56.

Arcana Imperii, secrets of State, by which it will proceed, and not be bound to *declare* them.[53]

After this statement of his physical condition, there is a brief attempt to try to see the situation in a more positive light. "But yet against those secret conspiracies in the State, the *Magistrate* hath the *rack*; and against the insensible diseases, *Phisicians* have their *examiners*; and those these employ now."[54] The extensive coping mechanisms of Meditations VI and VII are gone; even the repetitious examination and reassurance of Meditation VIII has stopped. Rather this is a statement of a serious condition without the usual flood of positive possibilities. The stage of using coping mechanisms to help handle anxiety is over. Although he continues to examine his situation, his conclusions cease to be positive. Meditations XI–XV reveal a man experiencing the advance of serious disease after the earlier emotional stages of anger and fear have given way to a state of increasing pessimism and despair.

Depression

In the five meditations that express Donne's depression, the use of coping mechanisms as a means of handling anxiety is the exception rather than the rule. Whereas in the sections on fear, Donne more or less successfully manages his distress by a process of separation, analyzation, and closure, this analyzation now actually reinforces his concern, so that the pattern here is one of increased hopelessness over the outcome of the illness with the closure now merely firming up the cause of despair.

Meditation XI is concerned with the doctor's attempt to keep the disease from advancing. "They use Cordials, to keep the venim and Malignitie of the disease from the Heart."[55] This treatment causes Donne to contemplate the phenomena of heart failure. Life is dependent on the functioning of the heart, he observes, and it is unfortunately, one of the most vulnerable organs. The brain or the liver "will endure a *Siege*; but an unnatural heat, a rebellious heat, will blow up the *heart*, like a *Myne*, in a *minute*."[56] This leads into a discussion of the frailty of man and the passage concludes with a reiteration of the beginning. "How little of a *Man* is the *Heart*, and yet it is all, by which he *is*; and this continually subject, not only to forraine poysons,

---

53. Donne, *Devotions* (Sparrow), 56.
54. Donne, *Devotions* (Sparrow), 56.
55. Donne, *Devotions* (Sparrow), 60.
56. Donne, *Devotions* (Sparrow), 61.

conveyed by others, but to intestine poysons, bred in ourselves by pestilentiall sicknesses."⁵⁷ Indeed, he has moved in the Meditation from seeing the heart as vulnerable to outside attack, to saying that the very person who is dependent on the heart, may be inadvertently responsible for its destruction. The closure here, takes the form of a lament over man's vulnerability. "O who, if before hee had a beeing, he could have sense of this miserie, would buy a being here upon these conditions."⁵⁸ Donne is expressing here his feelings of impotency over being dependent on a frail organ, his heart, for his life. These feelings of inability to effect a change or to act, are a recurring theme in the Meditations that follow.

Meditation XII again announces that its topic will evolve from a discussion of another form of treatment which the doctors have prescribed. "They apply Pidgeons, to draw the vapors from the Head."⁵⁹ This technique, common in the seventeenth century, causes Donne to think about what causes the vapors with which we "kill our selves."⁶⁰ He is told by the physicians that he has caused them by his own melancholy. Here we have a man who knows he is seriously ill and wishes to recover, being told that one of the reasons he is in danger is the presence of vapors in his head (a term of which he does not understand the meaning) and that he is himself causing these vapors by his own thoughtfulness. This makes him angry, and also despondent. "It is my *thoughtfulnesse*; was I not made to *thinke*? It is my *study*; doth not my *Calling* call for that? I have don nothing, wilfully, perversely toward it, yet must suffer in it, die by it."⁶¹ It is blaming the victim and serves to increase his feelings of helplessness and frustration. "What ill *ayre*, that I could have met in the street, what *Channell*, what *Shambles*, what *Dunghill*, what *vault*, could have hurt mee so much, as these home–bredd *vapours*?"⁶² At the end, the wistful hope surfaces again. "Be a good *Pigeon* to draw this *vapor* from the Head, and from doing any deadly harme there."⁶³

In Meditations XI and XII, Donne contemplates the frailty of life as seen in its dependency on the heart and the ability of the body itself, to aid in its own destruction. Critical days are sleepless days and nights, the passing of the hour an event. This theme of impotency and implication is interrupted by Meditation XIII, which is concerned with a new physical

---

57. Donne, *Devotions* (Sparrow), 63.
58. Donne, *Devotions* (Sparrow), 63.
59. Donne, *Devotions* (Sparrow), 67.
60. Bald, *Donne,* 452.; Donne, *Devotions* (Sparrow), 68.
61. Donne, *Devotions* (Sparrow), 69.
62. Donne, *Devotions* (Sparrow), 70.
63. Donne, *Devotions* (Sparrow), 70.

symptom, and its effect on the disease—i.e. "The Sicknes declares the infection and malignity thereof by spots."[64] This enables the physicians to make a diagnosis, but although Donne is glad to know the name of his illness, he gains small reassurance from this knowledge. "This sicknesse declares itself by *Spots*, to be a malignant, and pestilentiall disease, if there be a *comfort* in the declaration, that therby the *Phisicians* see more cleerely what to doe, there may bee as much *discomfort* in this, That the malignitie may bee so great, as that all that they can doe, shall doe *nothing*."[65] The analogies here again reinforce the pessimism: "That an enemy *declares* himself, then, when he is able to subsist, and to pursue, and to atchive his ends, is no great comfort . . . It is a faint comfort to know the worst, when the worst is *remedilesse*; and a weaker than that, to know *much ill*, and not to know, that that is the worst . . . O poore stepp toward being well, when these *spots* do only tell us, that we are worse, than we were sure of before."[66] The meditation ends in pessimism again. The brief comfort of knowing the diagnosis is lost in the flood of dismal conclusions. He now knows for certain that he has a very serious illness and that there is no sure cure. The final outcome of the disease is still unclear. Identifying the disease, then, has not lessened either his fear or his depression. It would seem, indeed, that he is using the knowledge to feed his own despair because he ignores the possible good signs and only examines the adverse ones.

Donne is now informed that his sickness has reached the critical days. Sparrow notes that "the fourth, fifth, seventh, ninth, eleventh, thirteenth, fourteenth, seventeenth, and twenty-first were supposed to be the 'critical days,' on which changes in a sick man's condition took place."[67] For his XIV Meditation, he uses this knowledge as a starting point for a discussion on the significance of time:

> What poore *Elements* are our *happinesses* made of, if *Tyme*, *Tyme* which wee can scarce consider to be any thing, be an essential part of our happines? . . . if we consider *Tyme* to be but the *Measure of Motion*, and howsoever it may seeme to have three *stations*, *past*, *present*, and *future*, yet the *first* and *last* of these *are* not (one is not, now, and the other is not yet) and that which you call *present*, is not *now* the same that it was, when you began to call it so in this *Line* . . . If this *Imaginary halfe-nothing*,

---

64. Donne, *Devotions* (Sparrow), 74.
65. Donne, *Devotions* (Sparrow), 74.
66. Donne, *Devotions* (Sparrow), 74–75.
67. Donne, *Devotions* (Sparrow), 151.

Tyme, be of the Essence of our *Happinesses*, how can they be thought *durable*?[68]

From this teaching of Saint Augustine's observations,[69] Donne moves on to observe that despite the elusiveness of time, there does seem to be such a thing as the right time for something to happen, which, if it happens later it loses its significance, such as a hot fire in the summer. He concludes this section by observing that "if happinesse be in the *season*, or in the *Clymate*, how much happier then are *Birdes* than *Men*, who can change the *Climate*, and accompanie, and enjoy the same season ever."[70]

This meditation, which poses the paradox of critical days in a world in which time is an illusion, seems strangely detached from the problems with which Donne has been working. However, when viewed in relationship to the sections that follow it, it becomes apparent that it is extremely significant, because it introduces and gives perspective to the time theme that Donne will work with in these meditations. As he becomes more depressed and increasingly ill, time and its measurement grow more and more important. Critical days are sleepless days and nights; the passing of the hour is an event to break the waiting, as is the passing of a man's life and the event of his death. All punctuate and anticipate the ever-present now of Donne's illness which occurs within a time structure that he acknowledges in this meditation to be illusory. It is as if when he is first ill, he is too preoccupied with the adaptation to and the management of his illness to contemplate final things, and that now, with this meditation, he is announcing a change in his orientation. Certainly, the dual significance of time will continue to reappear and to offer a tension to the events of the crisis.

In Meditation XV, Donne's depression, which began when medicines failed to cure and deepened after learning an unfavorable diagnosis, becomes acute: "I sleepe not day nor night . . . and oh, if I be entring now into *Eternitie*, where there shall bee no more distinction of *houres*, why is it al my businesse now *to tell Clocks*? why is none of the heavinesse of my *heart*, dispensed into mine *Eie-lids*, that they might fall as my heart doth? And why, since I have lost my delight in all objects, cannot I discontinue the facultie of seeing them, by closing mine *eies* in *sleepe*?"[71] This seems to be a description of an agitated depression, which combines fear and anxiety over his condition with acute pessimism over the prognosis, and frustration over his inability to influence his prognosis. He, himself, observes that

68. Donne, *Devotions* (Sparrow), 78–79.
69. Saint Augustine, *Confessions*, 260–62.
70. Donne, *Devotions* (Sparrow), 80.
71. Donne, *Devotions* (Sparrow), 86–88.

he is no longer able to find the positive aspects of his condition. "But why rather being entring into that presence, where I shall wake continually and never sleepe more, doe I not interpret my continuall waking here, to bee a *parasceve*, and a *preparation* to that?"[72]

Acceptance

It is in this state of unrest, alone, bedridden, a prey to physical discomforts of his illness and mental anxiety over its outcome, that Donne begins his famous meditations on the significance of the tolling bells of the nearby church, meditations in which he reaches an acceptance of his situation. Meditation XVI marks a change in Donne's feeling state, although it continues the dramatic situation presented in Meditation XV. Donne is critically ill, bedridden, sleepless, and extremely alert mentally. In Meditation XV, however, he is still concerned—as he has been from the beginning of his illness—with himself, with all his energies focused on his own problems and how to cope with them. Specifically, he has just considered the literal problem of experiencing critical days and sleeplessness disturbed by clocks as it affects his own survival. Now, in his analysis of the tolling bells, although he relates their tolling to his own condition, he perceives this specifically as part of a common human experience that all men share and that unknown men are undergoing at that very moment. This relationship of his experiences to the suffering and death of others is announced in the meditation's heading: "From the Bells of the Church adjoyning, I am daily remembred of my buriall in the funeralls of others."[73]

Bells in the seventeenth century were used for many functions that we now delegate to the media of radio and television, newspaper, telephone, and internet. They signaled weddings, funerals, and other services; they marked the passage of time, and announced important secular events, such as victories and defeats in time of war. If you lived in a parish, its bells related to the events that occurred nearest to you. Specific bells were used for specific purposes, so that one could tell from the bell's sound what it was rung for.[74] The bell that Donne refers to in Meditation XVII is the Passing Bell, that was rung for the dying and that bell is to be distinguished from the bell that was tolled when someone died. The Sermon Bell which Donne also refers to in Meditation XVII "was rung in Pre–Reformation times to give

---

72. Donne, *Devotions* (Sparrow), 88.
73. Donne, *Devotions* (Sparrow), 91.
74. Papillon, "Bell," 373–74.

notice that a sermon was to be preached."[75] There were, of course, wedding bells, bells for other specific services of the church, and within the church the celebration of the Holy Communion was preceded by a Sacrament Bell. Indeed, in the meditation which follows, it is interesting to observe that the ringing of a bell functions on this sacramental level also, as it is the outward sign that signifies Donne's recognition of a sense of community in his suffering.

As in all mutually shared customs, it was possible to move from parish to parish and recognize the information that the bells told; however, the bells of one's own parish had much more meaning because the people knew the other parishioners and were able to link specific individuals with the information. Thus Donne, in Meditation XVI, observes that "I have heard both *Bells* and *Ordnance*, but never been so much affected with those, as with these *Bells*. I have *lien* near a *Steeple*, in which there are said to be more than *thirty Bels*; And neere another, where there is one so bigge, as that the *Clapper* is said to weigh more than *six hundred pound*, yet never so affected as here. Here the *Bells* can scarse solemnise the funerall of any person, but that I knew him, or knew that he was my *Neighbor*: we dwelt in houses neere to one another."[76] His subsequent identification with his fellow parishioner's dying, then (although appropriately generalizable to all of humanity) is grounded in the many shared common experiences of daily life of his area in London, i.e. the same church, neighborhood, shops, and acquaintances. The funeral bells that announce the funerals of others are thus a reminder to Donne that he is not alone in his suffering, that he is still, although by himself, a part of a community of people, many of whom are also sharing his experience. He has previously identified with their vicissitudes, both in their faults and in misdeeds, "how many men that stand at an *execution*, if they would ask, for what dies that man, should heare their owne faults condemned, and see themselves executed, by *Atturney*?"[77] as well as in their successes, "We scarce heare any man *preferred*, but wee thinke of our selves, that wee might very well have beene that *Man*."[78] He can now identify with and learn from their dying. "When these *Bells* tell me, that now one, and now another is buried, must not I acknowledge, that they have the *correction* due to me, and paid the *debt* that I owe? . . . Why might not I have beene that *Man*, that is carried to his *grave* now?"[79] There is a recognition here of

75. Papillon, "Bell," 374.
76. Donne, *Devotions* (Sparrow), 92.
77. Donne, *Devotions* (Sparrow), 92.
78. Donne, *Devotions* (Sparrow), 92–93.
79. Donne, *Devotions* (Sparrow), 92–93.

the commonality of the situation he is in. It is a human experience, which all men share, and the appreciation of this community of suffering reassures him. "So when these hourely *Bells* tell me of so many *funerals* of men like me, it presents, if not a *desire* that it may, yet a *comfort* whensoever mine shall come."[80] Here, it is the sixteenth century meaning of comfort—i.e., to strengthen—that Donne means. He is strengthened as he shares others' suffering. Thus, the meditation ends, not in despair, but with a positive feeling of growth. The bells, which tell him of the funerals of other people in this area, have made him aware that he is not alone in this illness.

Physical isolation combined with tremendous psychological involvement in his personal survival have heretofore blocked him from involvement with others; now he is aware that others are also suffering, and he gains psychological strength from this awareness. There is no further attempt to control the situation; the extensive concern for himself has given way to accepting the situation and trying to understand its significance.

In Meditation XVII, Donne continues to work with this interrelationship of his suffering. "Now, this Bell tolling softly for another, saies to me, Thou must die."[81] The heading, which is in the preceding meditation, refers to the bells in general, now centers upon one specific passing bell; Donne contemplates the similarities between his situation and *one* other person who lies dying not far away. He observes that the unknown person may be so ill that he does not know that the passing bell is being rung for him. "Perchance hee for whom this *Bell* tolls, may be so ill, as that he knowes not it tolls for him."[82] Indeed, it is possible that Donne does not realize how sick he is and that the bell is being rung for him. "Perchance I may thinke my selfe so much better than I am, as that they who are about mee, and see my state, may have caused it to toll for mee, and I know not that."[83] This original premise and its implications are then analyzed for the rest of the meditation. Just as the passing bell, being rung for one person, affects all the sick, the events that happen to individuals within the community of the Church, affect all members. Examples are given of a baptism and a funeral. "The *Church* is *Catholike, universall,* so are all her *Actions; All* that she does, belongs to *all.* When she *baptizes a child,* that action concernes mee; for that child is thereby connected to that *Head* which is my *Head* too, and engraffed into that *body,* whereof I am a *member.* And when she *buries a Man,* that

---

80. Donne, *Devotions* (Sparrow), 93.
81. Donne, *Devotions* (Sparrow), 96.
82. Donne, *Devotions* (Sparrow), 96.
83. Donne, *Devotions* (Sparrow), 96–97.

action concernes me."[84] This interrelationship of specific events is also seen in the sermon bell, that calls "not upon the *Preacher* onely, but upon the *Congregation* to come" and this brings home again the message of the passing bell "so this *Bell* calls us all: but how much more mee, who am brought so neere the *doore* by this *sicknesse*."[85] Here Donne, having established the fact that all men may be influenced by events that would appear to affect only particular people, moves on to the concept that certain events have more meaning for people who are closest to the experience themselves, and who are personally able to recognize the relationship of their own situation to that of another. "The *Bell* doth toll for him that *thinkes* it doth; and though it *intermit* againe, yet from that *minute*, that that occasion wrought upon him, hee is united to *God*."[86] The recognition of the commonality of human experience thus moves to unite man to God, a unity which is achieved not by removal from the world but by an identification with other people in the world. This is not the way of a Saint Teresa or a Saint John of the Cross, but rather Jesus of Nazareth who ministered through human relationships. The difference in our response to the rising sun and to a comet is given as an example of the particular ability of certain events to speak to certain people. "Who casts not up his *Eie* to the *Sunne* when it rises? but who takes off his *Eie* from a *Comet* when that breakes out?"[87] Thus, "who bends not his *eare* to any *bell*, which upon any occasion rings? but who can remove it from that *bell*, which is passing a *peece of himselfe* out of this *world*?"[88] Then follows the famous description of the interrelationship of the particular man to all men: "No man is an *Iland*, intire of it selfe; every man is a peece of the *Continent*, a part of the *maine*; if a *Clod* bee washed away by the *Sea*, *Europe* is the lesse, as well as if a *Promontorie* were, as well as if a *Mannor* of thy *friends* or of *thine owne* were; any mans *death* diminishes *me*, because I am involved in *Mankinde*; And therefore never send to know for whom the *bell* tolls; It tolls for *thee*."[89]

This strong affirmation of his common humanity is the culmination of Donne's movement from the unidirectional concern for his personal survival to a recognition and an acceptance that his experience is shared by others in the community, who also suffer. As he accepts their suffering, he is able to accept his own situation. He is quick to point out that this identification

84. Donne, *Devotions* (Sparrow), 97.
85. Donne, *Devotions* (Sparrow), 97.
86. Donne, *Devotions* (Sparrow), 97.
87. Donne, *Devotions* (Sparrow), 97.
88. Donne, *Devotions* (Sparrow), 97–98.
89. Donne, *Devotions* (Sparrow), 98.

with other's sickness is not neurotic. "Neither can we call this a *begging* of *Miserie* or a *borrowing* of *Miserie*, as though we were not miserable enough of our selves, but must fetch in more from the next house, in taking upon us the *Miserie* of our *Neighbours*."[90] Rather, he states that personal growth results from being made aware of ultimate things as the suffering of others causes us to examine our own situation:[91] "No man hath *affliction* enough that is not matured, and ripened by it, and made fit for *God* by that *affliction* . . . Another man may be *sicke* too, and sick to *death*, and this *affliction* may lie in his *bowels*, as *gold* in a *Mine*, and be of no use to him; but this *bell*, that tells me of his *affliction*, digs out, and applies that *gold* to *mee*; if by this consideration of anothers danger, I take mine owne into contemplation, and so secure my selfe, by making my recourse to my *God*, who is our onely securitie."[92] At this point, Donne is no longer trying to change his state of illness. His hostility to his enforced sick–role behavior, as seen in his complaints about being bedridden, having to depend on a doctor, and being left alone, and his consuming interest in the course of the illness, whose advances he first meets with coping mechanisms and then with the impotency of acute depression, have ended. He now accepts his situation and having accepted it he is able to use the experience as an opportunity for personal growth—for contemplation of its meaning for him and for other men.

Just as in Meditation VIII where Donne affirms the experience of recognizing wholeness of self and the desire to share this feeling with others who also have experienced it, he now affirms the growth that comes from a recognition of and a sharing in human suffering. He has previously been too concerned with the improvement of his situation to experience this phenomenon—now, however, through his sense of community with others, he is able to benefit from the experience, to concentrate on the message of shared suffering, as it reaffirms his place in the universe. This is a wholeness of view, which sees the total event, yet rejects nothing and rationalizes nothing while "making my recourse to my *God*, who is our onely securitie."[93] Thus, Donne has moved from a man whose entire world was built on his own personal control of health and of external events—whose center was set awry by an illness beyond this control and whose resulting anxiety and emotional stress emphasized this loss of stability in his fierce struggle to regain it—to a person who is aware that this security he seeks lies in seeing himself as a human being subject to human experience and whose ultimate

---

90. Donne, *Devotions* (Sparrow), 98.
91. Tillich, *Dynamics of Faith*, 1–28.
92. Donne, *Devotions* (Sparrow), 98.
93. Donne, *Devotions* (Sparrow), 98.

concern is his relationship to God as reflected in his relationship to his neighbor, which offers the security that he had previously sought to achieve through personal control.

At this point, it is necessary to discuss briefly the role of the other two parts of Donne's *Devotions,* which have not been analyzed so far. Following each Meditation, Donne has a second section called an Expostulation, which continues on a spiritual level the treatment of a subject previously introduced in the Meditation. For example, in the second Meditation, Donne describes the suddenness of his physical illness. In the Expostulation, he examines what this illness could mean in terms of his spiritual relationship with God. He observes that all things come from God and that therefore his illness must have been sent as a sign of God's anger or hopefully only of God's correction. After this analysis, Donne ends the Devotion with a Prayer, which offers some closure on the situation by asking God to help him understand what his sickness means. In the earlier Devotions, he consistently separates his spiritual insights from his more secular observations, so that it may be said that he works through a specific problem on two different planes in each exercise—exhibiting the same dualism in approach that has been observed by many critics in his poetry. It is this dualism that makes a separate analysis of the early Meditations possible, even though additional insights are found in the Expostulations and Prayers. As his illness reaches the crisis which is described in Meditations XVI, XVII, and XVIII, however, it is interesting to note that the dualistic approach that has been maintained thus far is no longer existent. Instead, the Meditation, Expostulation, and Prayer exhibit a fusion of theme that seems to reinforce the wholeness of insight and direction that is achieved by Donne in these sections. Specifically, in Meditation XVII, Donne is drawn by the tolling of the passing bell to a recognition of a shared suffering. In the Expostulation that follows, he continues his discussion of sharing suffering by questioning why God uses this method for growth more than a more joyful means; and after resolving the question, he goes on to the Prayer, in which he prays for the person who is dying. This concern for others, which is new in these two meditations, is equally new to his expostulations. Previously he has related his physical illness to a spiritual problem that concerns him, and his prayers have been for himself. Now, however, we have Donne thinking of another man and praying for him. Before, also, he has often removed the Expostulation and Prayer from the immediate event. Now, they are concerned with the same problems as the Meditation and with the same immediacy. Thus, the union of physical and spiritual experience reflects Donne's sense of communion with man and God.

In Meditation XVIII we are told that "the Bell rings out, and tells me in him, that I am dead."[94] The passing bell has given way to the funeral bell, "The *pulse* thereof is changed; the *tolling* was a *faint*, and *intermitting pulse*, upon one side; this *stronger*, and argues *more* and *better life*."[95] The bell's announcement of death leads Donne to contemplate the fate of the man's soul—its origin and its future welfare. "It is the *going out*, more than the *comming in*, that concernes us. This *soule*, this Bell tells me, is *gone out*; *Whither*? Who shall tell mee that?"[96] Although he does not know, has not seen the course of his life, and has not been physically present at his death, Donne feels that "*he is gone to everlasting rest*, and *joy*, and *glory*."[97] He believes this because he has prayed for him as he lay dying and because the man had spoken to Donne's own problem through the passing bell: "I owe him a good *opinion*; it is but *thankfull charity* in mee, because I received *benefit* and *instruction* from him when his *Bell* told: and I, being made the fitter to *pray*, by that disposition, wherein I was assisted by his occasion, did *pray* for him; and I *pray* not without *faith*; so I doe *charitably*, so I do *faithfully* beleeve, that that *soule* is gone to everlasting *rest*, and *joy*, and *glory*."[98] This again reaffirms Donne's new participation in the human community. This unknown man has helped him, and Donne, through his love for him that is actualized in his prayers, has reciprocated with his own help.

After this section, there follows a passage in which Donne mourns over the mutability of the body in contrast to the spirit. "Who would not bee affected, to see a cleere and sweet *River* in the *Morning*, grow a *kennell* of muddy land water by *noone*, and condemned to the saltnesse of the *Sea* by *night*? And how lame a *picture*, how faint a *representation* is that, of the precipitation of mans body to dissolution?"[99] It is an expression of grief, which is experienced by all men, and which Donne is able to verbalize at the same time that he is affirming the continuity of the man's soul.

---

94. Donne, *Devotions* (Sparrow), 102.
95. Donne, *Devotions* (Sparrow), 102.
96. Donne, *Devotions* (Sparrow), 104.
97. Donne, *Devotions* (Sparrow), 104.
98. Donne, *Devotions* (Sparrow), 104.
99. Donne, *Devotions* (Sparrow), 105.

Motif of Time

The motif of time, which was introduced in Meditation XIV, has run throughout the meditations which follow. Certainly, Donne's cry of "oh, if I be entring now into *Eternitie*, where there shall bee no more distinction of *houres*, why is it al my businesse now *to tell Clocks*?" has been answered in a paradoxical form worthy of his own structuring.[100] The bells, which signal earthly events—the hours, the ecclesiastical offices, and occurrences within the life of the parish—are indeed vehicles which mark the passage of time on this earth. First communions, marriage, death—these bells announce the various stages of man's life and in between these stages are the bells which sound the hours, both canonical and secular, announce the sermons, and the holy communion, and mark victories, defeats, coronations, and national emergencies. Thus, the ringing of bells was almost synonymous with the passage of time and so with earthly events. Yet it is in one of these moments, when the passing bell is tolling for a dying parishioner who is moving in time from life to death, that Donne experiences an acceptance of his humanity and an awareness of God that is eternal. "The *Bell* doth toll for him that *thinkes* it doth; and though it *intermit* againe, yet from that *minute*, that that occasion wrought upon him, hee is united to *God*."[101] The occurrence, then, that is a very part of the business of time itself, has moved Donne to empathize with his neighbor, to apprehend that he is a part of an experience common to all men that is in itself timeless. And with that apprehension of the eternal now of suffering,[102] he is able to escape the burden of the uncertainties of becoming and experience the comfort of ultimacy—of "*God*, who is our onely securitie."[103]

This contemplation of the eternal, however, does not remove Donne from participating in a world of time. Rather, it is only after his acceptance of his human situation, in which his role is to suffer, not act, that he is able to act in a meaningful way. He is still impotent to change his own situation; in his condition, he can neither treat, prescribe, nor will a physical response to treatment. In fact, he has recognized that his own desire and concern to control the illness may be causing anxiety that advances the disease. He *is* capable, now, of concern for other men in his situation.[104] He prays for the man who is dying and feels assured that his prayers have helped effect that

---

100. Donne, *Devotions* (Sparrow), 88.
101. Donne, *Devotions* (Sparrow), 97.
102. Tillich, *Dynamics of Faith*, 1–28.
103. Donne, *Devotions* (Sparrow), 98.
104. Andreasen, "Psychology of Assent," 215–16.

man's "everlasting *rest*, and *joy*, and *glory*."[105] As he accepts his full humanity, against which he has fought up until this time, for it means his acceptance of disease, sickness, and death—those temporal occurrences which all men fear—he is able to participate in those human concerns that are timeless: empathy with his fellow men who also suffer and rejoice, love for them, and right action growing from that empathetic love.

It is in that spirit that Donne contemplates the dissolution of the body after death. There are none of the old feelings of hostility and depression stemming from impotence here. It is honest grief, for the rapid decay of a form which has been familiar and loved. This contemplation of mortality and decay, certainly a temporal subject appropriate for the ending of this section on time, is a touchstone for how rapidly Donne has moved in his thought. There are no exclamations against the event, no coping mechanisms to help him handle the unbearable thought of dissolution. Instead, there is an accurate description of physiological phenomenon, which is accepted for what it is—a natural event. "In the wombe of the *earth*, wee *diminish*, and when shee is *deliverd* of us, our *grave opened* for another, wee are not *transplanted*, but *transported*, our *dust* blowne away with *prophane dust*, with *every wind*."[106] It does not have to do with the business of being human, to which Donne has been restored.

Hope

With Meditation XIX, there is a sharp break in the feeling tone. Donne is back again, recounting the events of his illness, observing his doctors, introducing analogies to help him understand and express his feelings. The moment of the bells is ended. But the approach to his sickness and the feeling tone of the meditation is remarkably anxiety free. "At last, the Physitians, after a long and stormie voyage, see land; They have so good signes of the concoction of the disease, as that they may safely proceed to purge."[107] There is no questioning of their ability, no hesitancy over their choice of treatment, no fear of their choice of medicine. There is no statement of his own impotency. The situation is still described objectively, yet there is a decided feeling of optimism:

> All this while, therefore, we are but upon a *defensive warre*, and that is but a *doubtfull state*; especially where they who are

---

105. Donne, *Devotions* (Sparrow), 104.
106. Donne, *Devotions* (Sparrow), 105.
107. Donne, *Devotions* (Sparrow), 110.

> *besieged* doe know the *best* of their *defences*, and doe not know the *worst* of their *enemies power*; when they cannot mend their *works within*, and the *enemie* can increase his *numbers without*. O how many farre more miserable, and farre more worthy to be lesse miserable than I, are besieged with this *sicknesse*, and lacke their *Sentinels*, their *Physitians* to *watch*, and lacke their *munition*, their *cordials* to *defend*, and perish before the *enemies* weaknesse might invite them to *sally*, before the *disease* shew any *declination*, or admit any way of *working* upon it selfe? In me the *siege* is so farre slackned, as that we may come to *fight*, and so die in the *field*, if I *die*, and not in a *prison*.[108]

Using battle imagery, he compares his previous condition to a state of siege, which has been maintained by the able assistance of his doctors, and which now has lessened enough for him to put up a fight in the field. The resolution, the sense of action, and the generally improved outlook of Donne fill this Meditation with hope. Although he will continue to experience moments of anger, depression, and fear, as his convalescence continues, this positive outlook sets the general tone for the rest of the meditations. It is not false optimism—he recognizes that he may "die in the *field*"[109]—but it is a mood free of the over-anxious concern of the first part of the illness.

Emotions During Convalescence

Meditations XX–XXIII may be grouped together, as they are each concerned with some problem of convalescence. After the high drama of the illness, with its anger, loneliness, fear, and depression culminating in the intense emotional experience of the bells that mark Donne's acceptance of his illness and followed by Meditation XIX, heady with its expressed hope, these may seem anticlimactic and even disappointing in their revelation of the foibles still to be found in Donne's behavior. Certainly, in force of dramatic interest, they suffer by comparison with the previous meditations. Yet the work, as a whole, gains by their inclusion. In them we see that the Donne who has experienced rapid growth in time of crisis, must continue to work on his assimilation of these insights into his daily life. And just because he has had the experience, this does not mean that he will always be so open to the eternal. He is accustomed to a lifetime of controlling behavior, and it will reappear, to be worked through again and again. This, too, however, is as much a part of the human experience as is the moment of crisis. We can

---

108. Donne, *Devotions* (Sparrow), 112.
109. Donne, *Devotions* (Sparrow), 112.

identify with Donne's daily frustrations—they help us see and accept him as a real person—for we have all had encounters with ultimacy, only to follow the less admirable course afterwards.

Meditation XX is concerned with Donne's reaction to the doctor's decision to purge him. "Upon these Indications of digested matter, they proceed to purge"[110] Although the tone is one of trust in his doctors— "Without *counsell*, I had not got thus farre; without *action* and *practise*, I should goe no farther towards *health*"[111]—Donne objects to the immediate remedy. "But what is the present necessary *action*? purging: A *withdrawing*, a violating of *Nature*."[112] He is angry that they have decided to do this to him. Certainly, the modern hospital patient, who has experienced the battery of tests attendant with almost the slightest problem will empathize with Donne's questioning the need for one more series.

Meditation XXI is largely a description of Donne's physical condition during convalescence. Specifically, it relates to the occasion of his leaving his bed. "God prospers their practise, and he, by them, calls Lazarus out of his tombe, mee out of my bed."[113] Again, there is the allusion, made by the connection with Lazarus, to Donne's apprehension of the bed as a grave. And again, just as going to bed makes him aware of his dependent situation, so trying to get up also raises his awareness of his need for help. "I cannot *rise* out of my bed, till the *Physitian enable* mee, nay I cannot tel, that I am able to rise, till *hee tell* me so. I *doe* nothing, I *know* nothing of myselfe: how little, and how impotent a peece of the *world*, is any *Man* alone? and how much lesse a peece of *himselfe* is *that Man*?"[114] Several trends should be noted here. First of all, Donne is here being called upon to adapt to a new situation again in which his dependency is obvious. He is having trouble with this adaptation, just as he did before—both with the dependent state, which he resists, and the change in behavior, which he also resists. The same feelings of impotency surface to be worked through once more. The difficulty in changing his status will recur throughout the remaining meditations. "Another tels mee, *I may rise*; and I *doe* so. But is every *raising* a *preferment*? or is every present *preferment* a *station*? I am readier to fall to the *Earth*, now I am up, than I was when I *lay* in the bed."[115] Thus, he seems to have some problem giving up the sick role and adapting to the responsibility of normal life, just as he had

---

110. Donne, *Devotions* (Sparrow), 120.
111. Donne, *Devotions* (Sparrow), 121.
112. Donne, *Devotions* (Sparrow), 121.
113. Donne, *Devotions* (Sparrow), 126.
114. Donne, *Devotions* (Sparrow), 127.
115. Donne, *Devotions* (Sparrow), 127.

trouble adapting to the sick role earlier. He describes his physical weakness: "I am *up*, and I seeme to *stand*, and I goe *round*; and I am a new *Argument* of the *new Philosophie*, That the *Earth* moves round; why may I not beleeve, that the *whole earth* moves in a *round motion*, though that seeme to mee to *stand*, when as I seeme to *stand* to my *Company*, and yet am carried, in a giddy, and *circular motion*, as I *stand*? Man hath no *center* but *misery*."[116] Donne is back lamenting man's sorry state, and this after his time of awareness! The old patterns are there, easily repeated, only changed with much work. "Every thing serves to *exemplifie*, to *illustrate* mans *misery*. But I need goe no farther, than *my selfe*: for a long time, I was not able to *rise*; At last, I must bee *raised* by others; and now I am *up*, I am ready to sinke *lower* than before."[117]

In Meditation XXII, Donne continues to respond to his treatment with feelings of impotency which inevitably leave him depressed. This section in which "the Physitians consider the root and occasion, the embers, and coales, and fuell of the disease, and seeke to purge or correct that" follows the general pattern of Meditation IV, in which Donne discusses the lack of self-sufficiency in man, who must call in a physician to treat his illness.[118] Now, he explores that dependency on medication derived from external sources, rather than from within: "Where the *ground* cannot give it selfe *Physicke*, yet it receives *Physicke* from other grounds, from other soiles, which are not the worse, for having contributed that helpe to them . . . But I have taken a *farme* at this *hard rent*, and upon those *heavie covenants*, that it can afford it selfe no *helpe*; (no part of my *body*, if it were cut off, would *cure* another part) . . . There is nothing in the same *man*, to help *man*."[119] Once again, he is aware of his lack of self-sufficiency and in comparing man to inhuman things, comes away depressed.

Finally, in the last meditation, fear, another emotion that was experienced in the earlier sections, surfaces once more. "They warne mee of the fearefull danger of relapsing."[120] In another advance toward a return to well behavior, Donne has been given responsibility for his health, a responsibility he very much resented relinquishing. Now, however, he is apprehensive over resuming this charge and is fearful that he may have another attack. "It is not in *mans body*, as it is in the *Citie*, that when the *Bell* hath rung, to cover your *fire*, and rake up the *embers*, you may lie downe and sleepe without feare. Though you have by *physicke* and *diet*, raked up the *embers*

---

116. Donne, *Devotions* (Sparrow), 128.
117. Donne, *Devotions* (Sparrow), 128.
118. Donne, *Devotions* (Sparrow), 133.
119. Donne, *Devotions* (Sparrow), 135.
120. Donne, *Devotions* (Sparrow), 139.

of your *disease*, stil there is a feare of a *relapse*; and the *greater* danger is in that."[121] This fear of relapse is worse, says Donne, than an apprehension of the original disease, whose effects were previously unknown to him. One must actually experience the disease to truly sympathize with others who suffer from it. "*Diseases*, which we never *felt* in our selves, come but to a *compassion* of others that have endured them; Nay, *compassion* it selfe comes to no great *degree*, if wee have not felt in some *proportion*, in *our selves*, that which wee lament and condole in another. But when wee have had those torments in their *exaltation, our selves*, wee tremble at a relapse."[122] Added to the misery of being able to predict just how bad the disease is, is the unpredictability of the outcome of these known miseries. "When wee must stand at the same *barre*, expect the returne of *Physitians* from their *consultations*, and not bee sure of the same *verdict*, in any good *Indications*, when we must goe the same *way* over againe, and not see the same *issue*, this is a *state*, a *condition*, a *calamitie*, in respect of which, any other *sicknesse*, were a *convalescence*, and any *greater, lesse*."[123]

Finally, the event of a relapse is often blamed upon the person who is suffering from it. "It addes to the *affliction*, that *relapses* are, (and for the most part justly) imputed to *our selves*, as occasioned by some *disorder* in us; and so we are not onely *passive*, but *active*, in our owne *ruine*."[124] These reasons why one has a right to fear a relapse, which Donne gives to help him cope with his own fear, follow the same sort of pattern that he uses in his essay on fear in Meditation VI. Again, we are so aware of his sharp powers of observation, which make such a logical case for his emotion, that we almost lose sight of the necessity for this analysis—i.e. to handle his own anxiety. The final sentence, however, which is the summation of his examination, moves back to a statement of his fear—which is not allayed by all the preceding assurances. "Upon a *sicknesse*, which as yet appeares not, wee can scarce fix a *feare*, because wee know not what to feare; but as *feare* is the *busiest*, and *irksomest affection*, so is a *relapse* (which is still *ready to come*) into that, which is but newly gone, the *nearest object*, the *most immediate* exercise of that *affection* of *feare*."[125] The meditation ends, then, not on a note of resolution of conflict, but in the midst of Donne's continued struggle with new situations, which brings up old anxieties, to be worked through again.

---

121. Donne, *Devotions* (Sparrow), 139–40.
122. Donne, *Devotions* (Sparrow), 140.
123. Donne, *Devotions* (Sparrow), 140–41.
124. Donne, *Devotions* (Sparrow), 141.
125. Donne, *Devotions* (Sparrow), 141.

Summary

Thus, an analysis of John Donne's account of his critical illness of 1623 reveals a series of psychological stages which he experiences in the course of that illness. His anger over being bed-ridden, dependent on the doctor, and abandoned by his friends; his loneliness; his fear over the possible outcome of the disease, which surfaces one step removed in his anxieties over the doctor's treatment and is coped with through complex intellectualizations; and his subsequent depression as the disease continues to advance, are all carefully described. His acceptance of his illness and his renewed hope for a cure, all come out in his detailed record of this time of crisis. During his convalescence, he again is seen to experience situations to which he responds with anger, depression, and fear, and the mechanisms he uses to express and handle these feelings follow the patterns he has used in his illness.

Having defined these emotions, further study of their dynamics leads to a psychological examination of Donne's sick role behavior, an examination of the particular emotional states that Donne experiences when he is critically ill, and a comparison of these states to those studied by thanatologists today. These same dynamics suggest an examination of Donne's emotional evolution from self-centered to other-centered behavior in light of the theology of Paul Tillich. Finally, an examination of Donne's life history in search of possible causes for his great distress when illness interrupts his life, gives further insight into his behavior. These studies, although separated for analysis, all interrelate and are all subject to the same basic structure which grows out of the emotional evolution which has been presented in the preceding progression of described feeling states. Therefore, before beginning the several analyses that have been suggested here, it is appropriate to look at this overall structure of the *Devotions upon Emergent Occasions*.

Part II

The Structure of the *Devotions:* Adaptation to Change

To make my self believe that our life is something, I use my thoughts to compare it to something, if it be like any thing that is something. It is like a Sentence, so much as may be uttered in a breathing: and such a difference as is in Styles, is in our lives, contracted and dilated. And as in some Styles, there are open Parentheses, Sentences within Sentences; so there are lives, within our lives. I am in such a Parenthesis now, in a convalescence, when I thought my self verie near my period. God brought me into a low valley, and from thence shewed me high *Jerusalem*, upon so high a hill, as that he thought it fit to bid me stay, and gather more breath. This I do, by meditating by expostulating, by praying; for, since I am barred of my ordinarie diet, which is Reading, I make these my exercises, which is another part of Physick.
"To a Lord, Upon Presenting of Some of His Work to Him,"
JOHN DONNE, 1624[1]

---

1. Coffin, *Complete Poetry*, 395–96.

Structure of the Entire Work: Relationship to Donne's Emotional States

John Donne's *Devotions upon Emergent Occasions* contains twenty-three Devotions, each subdivided into two headings: a Latin and an English; and three sections: a Meditation, an Expostulation, and a Prayer, which were written during the course of a critical illness and which are concerned with specific aspects of that illness. They are unified overtly by their basic uniform structure, and the common occasion of their composition. Like style, imagery, and viewpoint offer further cohesiveness. The progression of the illness itself also serves as a unifying force. When, however, the work is examined in relationship to the feeling states that are exhibited in the work, their organization, and evolution, it is apparent that they outline an internal structuring for the entire work which transcends the twenty-three separate parts and gives a new vehicle for the interpretation of that work.

Basically, this structure in which Donne's emotions are so important is built on a change from an old order to a new order and a return to that old order again. In this process of change, disorder is experienced each time before the new state is fully incorporated. It is in his working through this demanded reorientation that Donne experiences the psychological states of anger, loneliness, fear, depression, acceptance, and hope that are described in Part One. In Meditation I, Donne's strong reaction to the sudden alteration in his health brought on by a precipitous illness is initially one that cries out against change. "Variable, and therfore miserable condition of Man; this minute I was well, and am ill, this minute."[2] Thus, changeableness is equated with misery, and misery is equated with disorder: "We study *Health*, and we deliberate upon our *meats*, and *drink*, and *ayre*, and *exercises*, and we hew, and wee polish every stone, that goes to that building; and so our *Health* is a long and a regular work; But in a minute a Canon batters all, overthrowes all, demolishes all; a *Sicknes* unprevented for all our diligence, unsuspected for all our curiositie; nay, undeserved, if we consider only *disorder*, summons us, seizes us, possesses us, destroyes us in an instant. O miserable condition of Man."[3]

This flashback to the carefully organized and regulated life that Donne perceives himself experiencing prior to the onset of illness is the first in a series of references that he makes to his former healthy state. In these references, we are able to gain some idea of the premium that Donne places on his old environment, on being independent, self-sufficient, and controlling

---

2. Donne, *Devotions* (Sparrow), 1.
3. Donne, *Devotions* (Sparrow), 1.

the course of events. Whether or not this is idealized behavior, Donne wishes to return to the old order and it is only at the end of sixteen meditations, having worked through strong feelings of anger, loneliness, fear, and depression over his condition that he is able to accept the new order that demands both a relinquishing of control over the events that shape his life and a dependency on others. Having accepted this new order, however, Donne goes through another period of adjustment when he is called upon to return to the old order that existed prior to the illness. Again, a change brings disorder and reorientation that is still going on when the *Devotions* end.

A major theme, then, of these *Devotions upon Emergent Occasions* is neither a vindication of self-reliance, nor conversely, of dependency; but rather, a presentation of the phenomena that occur when a person is called upon to accept change—in this particular incident, the change demanded by a sudden and critical illness. Whether it is the adaptation to the sick role, the adaptation to a dying state, or the adaptation to a different relationship with God, change makes for emotional response that must be worked through before any real acceptance may be reached. After this structure of old order → disorder → new order → disorder → old order is understood, sociological, psychological, theological, and psychoanalytical interpretations may be made in line with that structure, working across the individual meditations in a consideration of the work as a whole.

Structure of Individual *Devotions*: Expression of Donne's Coping Techniques

If a structure for the total work grows from an examination of Donne's emotional responses throughout an illness, the converse is true of the structure of the individual devotions, for it is through an examination of this overt organization that Donne's technique for handling his emotions and relating to God and man is revealed. Van Laan has previously noted the similarities of these exercises to the form of a Jesuit meditation.[4] The use of a heading to limit the subject for meditation, the division of each Devotion into three parts, in which the meditation relates to a physical aspect of the problem, the expostulation relates to the spiritual aspects, and the prayer offers a resolution of the problem, were also characteristics of a Jesuit exercise, and Donne, a relative of Sir Thomas More, raised in the Roman Catholic Church in England, and an early witness to its persecution by Elizabeth, was certainly acquainted with the form and its use. Its patterns have been recognized by

---

4. Van Laan, "Jesuit Spiritual Exercises," 191–202.

Martz and Gardner in the structuring of his poetry, as well as his prose.[5] It is a form particularly suited to Donne, who consistently presents a dualistic message, and its adaptation here yields significant insight into Donne's cross meditation technique for dealing with emotions. It is a five-part approach in which Donne deals with a feeling state through: 1. an identification of a problem; 2. a fragmentation into different areas of life of the emotion that occurs in response to the problem; 3. a farther compartmentalization of the problem within secular and religious lines; 4. an attempt to cope with the emotion on these two different planes through intellectualization that may take the form of analogies, analyses, or examples (he has himself described this technique of using analogies in his letter to the Lord, Upon Presenting of Some of His Work to Him: "To make myself believe that our life is something, I use in my thoughts to compare it to something, if it be like anything that is something."[6]); and finally 5. the achievement of some sort of closure, again on two levels.

For example, in Meditation VI, Donne announces in the two headings that he is dealing with the problems raised by the physician's fear. After this identification, he begins the meditation, in which fear is analyzed from the aspect of physical phenomena. He carefully describes the situation: "I observe the *Phisician*, with the same diligence, as hee the *disease*; I see hee *feares*, and I feare with him . . . He knowes that his *feare* shall not disorder the practise, and exercise of his *Art*, but he knows that my *fear* may disorder the effect, and working of his practise."[7] Thus, he has narrowed the subject to a consideration of why the doctor wishes to keep Donne from feeling anxiety. Having limited the area to be discussed, Donne proceeds to intellectualize on fear, its manifestations and stimulation. He compares it to the way hyperventilation may produce psychosomatic symptoms—"the *wind* in the body will counterfet any disease."[8] Love of having may really be a fear of losing, brave acts may occur not from courage but from fear of peer group disapproval. Fear may be aroused by objects that do not warrant the anxiety—i.e. irrational fear: "A man that is not afraid of a *Lion* is afraid of a *Cat*; not afraid of *starving*, and yet is afraid of some *joynt of meat* at the table, presented to feed him."[9] Then, having examined the manifestations of fear and the irrationality of it, in depth, he concludes that "I know not,

---

5. Martz, *The Poetry of Meditation*.; Gardner, *Divine Poems*.
6. Coffin, *Complete Poetry*, 395.
7. Donne, *Devotions* (Sparrow), 28.
8. Donne, *Devotions* (Sparrow), 28.
9. Donne, *Devotions* (Sparrow), 28.

what fear is, nor I know not what it is that I fear now."[10] Now follow several analyses of what he perceives that he does and does not fear, and finally, the meditation is ended with an attempt at resolution: "but as my *Phisicians* fear puts not him from his *practise*, neither doth mine put me, from receiving from *God*, and *Man*, and *my selfe*, *spirituall*, and *civill*, and *morall* assistances, and consolations."[11] In the Expostulation, this same process of identification, fragmentation, intellectualization, and closure is followed on a spiritual level: "They j*oy* in thee, *O Lord*, that *feare* thee, and *feare* thee only, who feele this j*oy in thee*. Nay, thy *feare* and thy *love*, are inseparable; still we are called upon, in infinite places, to *feare God*; yet the *Commandement*, which is the r*oote* of all, is, *Thou shalt love the Lord thy God*; Hee doeth *neither*, that doth not *both*; hee omits *neither*, that does *one*."[12]

Finally, the prayer, which offers closure for the entire devotion, follows the same internal structure. A specific quality of God is addressed and help is asked for a specific problem, which is elaborated on and further defined before closing: "Let mee not therefore, *O my God*, bee ashamed of these *feares*, but let me feele them to determine, where his feare did, in a present submitting of all to thy will."[13]

We see, then, a gross pattern that is established in the form of the *Devotions*, that is repeated in the three major parts of that exercise: the meditation, the expostulation, and the prayer, and that may be used as a further technique for analyzing specific issues within an individual section. This technical method for establishing order and achieving intellectual control over a threatening situation is helpful to Donne as he works through crises.[14] It keeps him from disintegrating from nonspecific anxiety under the bombardment of new stimuli. As a coping mechanism, then, it is successful in helping structure an unknown environment. It is not, however, effective in dealing with the cause of his anxiety, the need to adapt to his changed condition, and thus he repeats his formula for control over and over again as new emotional responses occur, until he reaches an acceptance of his situation and does not perceive his milieu as a hostile environment. When this acceptance does occur, the formula becomes altered. Although the form of meditation, expostulation, and prayer are continued overtly, they are united into an ongoing process in which the physical and spiritual separation of a problem are replaced by the continued concern of Donne for his dying

---

10. Donne, *Devotions* (Sparrow), 28.
11. Donne, *Devotions* (Sparrow), 29.
12. Donne, *Devotions* (Sparrow), 33.
13. Donne, *Devotions* (Sparrow), 34.
14. Hunt, *Donne's Poetry*, 191–7.

neighbor for whom he prays in the prayer section. Thus, the wholeness of Donne's adaptation to his situation is reflected in the integration of the structure within the external parts of the *Devotions upon Emergent Occasions*. Later, when Donne is faced with a re-adaptation to normal behavior, the meditations grow apart from the expostulations once more. It is as if the intensity with which he uses the technique is indicative of his own lack of adjustment to the environment which he perceives he must then control as one would a hostile force.

It may be observed that the very discipline of writing these *Devotions* also serves as a structuring device for Donne, as does the discipline imposed by the form of the *Devotions* themselves. Certainly, an analysis of his poetry from this structural hypothesis would offer additional rich insights into this technique—as Donne consistently presents a situation in such a way as to appear to master it intellectually, and structurally, while the emotion, still there despite the exercise of will, spills out to challenge the reader and draw him to the personality of Donne—which is forever emotionally responsive and forever attempting to order these responses.

The preceding analysis of the cross-devotion significance of Donne's work within the Jesuit meditation form has briefly indicated the adaptability of this medium to the emotional comfort of the writer. Structurally rigid at the beginning, it becomes inter-related and flexible as Donne grows to accept his changed condition only to become restrictive once more when he moves toward normative behavior again.

The overall internal structure of the progressive emotional states experienced during the adaptive process that follows after a change has occurred, is thus reflected in the variations within the individual devotions form. As indicators of Donne's emotional adaptation, they may be interpreted for psychological, as well as for theological significance. In either analysis, however, it is important to remember that the use of structure within the individual devotions, sections of devotions, and segments of sections grows out of the need to cope with different feeling states that arise during a period of adaptation to a changed environment that is itself beyond Donne's control. The fact that he chooses to use the structure of the familiar form of a Jesuit meditation as a vehicle for his attempts to alleviate his discomfort is an example of the observed phenomena that in time of stress, we draw on past resources as means of coping.

Donne's early Roman Catholic experience and his immediate occupation as Dean of St. Paul's had thoroughly familiarized him with this devotional technique and made its incorporation natural. His feelings are universal, his particular expression of these feelings is intensely personal, partaking of his unique experience of Elizabethan and Stuart England. His years spent separate from the general milieu as a Roman Catholic, his European travel, his conversion to Anglicanism, his Renaissance education, budding career, ill–starred marriage, frustrated ambition, and final appointment to religious orders all influence his perception of his environment.

The methods he uses to cope in his illness repeat established patterns that have been used as defenses in other crises, and his intellectualizations are drawn from a multifaceted life experience. It is especially fortunate for us that during his life, John Donne had occasion to write both poetry and prose, for himself and for others, so that it was natural for him to choose to record the events of his illness, and to circulate this writing among his friends. This circumstance gives us the opportunity of following Donne's emotional state from the beginning of a critical illness until he is well into a convalescence. Not surprisingly, it has many similarities to the emotional states of dying patients observed by Dr. Elizabeth Kübler-Ross and described in her book, *On Death and Dying*, and it is instructive to begin a psychological examination of Donne's writing with a comparison of the two works.

Part III

Psychological, Sociological, Theological, and Psychoanalytical Studies Suggested by the Identification of Donne's Emotional States During Illness

No man is an Iland, entire of it selfe:

every man is a peece of the Continent, a part of the maine;

if a Clod bee washed away by the Sea, Europe is the lesse,

as well as if a Promontorie were,

as well as if a Mannor of thy friends or of thine owne were;

any mans death diminishes me, because I am involved in Mankinde;

And therefore never send to know for whom the bell tolls;

It tolls for thee.

—Meditation XVII, Devotions upon Emergent Occasions John Donne, 1623[1]

---

1. Donne, *Devotions* (Sparrow), 98.

Stages of Death and Dying, 1623–1973:
A Cross-cultural Study of Kübler-Ross and Donne

In his *Devotions upon Emergent Occasions*, John Donne describes his psychological responses to a critical illness—responses which parallel the psychological states that Dr. Elizabeth Kübler-Ross observed in her study of dying patients, *On Death and Dying*. Feelings of anger, loneliness, fear, and depression, intermingled with hope, and culminating in acceptance, feelings which have consistently recurred in Dr. Kübler-Ross's conversations with terminally ill patients, are also experienced by Donne. He shares with these patients the desire to communicate his feelings to others, and because he is a psychological poet and a priest–theologian whose university education has been broadened by continental travel, he brings to this communication a refinement of presentation and a complexity of insight that offers to the reader, today, a rare opportunity to see not only the way Donne feels in facing death, but how these basic emotions are integrated into his multifaceted personality. An analysis of Donne's feelings during this life crisis, and an examination of the way these emotions are handled and incorporated into the intricate microcosm that is Donne's world view, offers a fresh approach to the understanding of the poet himself, and furthermore, complements studies on the emotions of the hospitalized and the terminally ill patient; strengthening the basic observations of these studies through an identification of similar feelings experienced in another time and culture.

Background for Kübler-Ross Study

In 1965, Dr. Elizabeth Kübler-Ross, a psychiatrist at the University of Chicago, began a study of the emotional state of terminally ill patients in Billings Hospital. The study was undertaken in collaboration with the hospital chaplains, and its primary thrust was to learn firsthand from the dying themselves, how they felt about their situation. The work, which has become a prototype for subsequent investigations into the emotional state of various types of patients, had some difficulty in the beginning, because of a marked reticence among hospital personnel to talk with dying patients themselves. Some overt hostility from the staff was also encountered, and it was only after several tries that a patient was finally located who agreed to participate in the study. The patient, himself, however, proved eager to talk to the group about his feelings and this desire to communicate with others continued to be the norm for those patients who were interviewed. This interest in sharing emotions may have been reinforced by the fact that the hospital staff and even the patient's family tended to stay away from those patients who were identified as terminally ill. There seemed to be a taboo about mentioning the approaching death to them and often they were literally not allowed to share their anxieties with other people. Thus, the inquiries of Kübler-Ross's group served an unanticipated therapeutic function for the patients themselves.

The structure of the communication was in two stages: There was an initial interview in which the patient talked with Dr. Kübler-Ross and the chaplain about their particular case and about some of their emotions as they perceived them. This interview was followed by a second lengthy interview session, which was observed through a one-way mirror by the entire group. The group later followed up the interview with an analysis of the session. Problems suggested in the first session were discussed in depth by the patient, Dr. Kübler-Ross, and the chaplains. After this second interview, the patients were told that the group would be glad to work further with them individually on specific problems and depending on the nature and advancement of the illness, extended relationships with the patients were possible. As the study progressed, and patients responded favorably to the sessions, the group noticed a marked lessening of hostility on the part of the hospital staff, and finally, an imitation of the group's techniques was observed in the relationship of staff to patient.

Because the patients proved to be in different stages of working through to an acceptance of their illness, they tended at first to present different emotional responses to their death. As more patients were interviewed, however, certain emotional states began to recur, and in time, Dr. Kübler-Ross and her colleagues were able to definitely identify those emotional stages which a dying person experienced before they were able to reach an acceptance of their situation. These stages included denial, anger, bargaining, depression, and hope: the last state being present in all other stages to some extent. The maintenance of hope was not seen as a form of denial, but rather as a means of coping with feelings of despair. In her book *On Death and Dying*, Dr. Kübler-Ross gives extensive descriptions of each of these stages experienced by the terminally ill and illustrates these from actual interviews. While this analysis will not attempt to recapitulate those sessions, a brief summary of the major states is appropriate here.

Psychological Stages Experienced by Dying Patients

The first stage in that peculiar grief process which results from a person being told either overtly or covertly that they are terminally ill is one of shock followed by denial. This denial may take several forms—shopping for a doctor who will disagree with the diagnosis is very common; refusal to follow the physician's advice as to medication and diet is another easily recognized adaptation; failure to make plans to fulfill family duties in light of the illness and anticipated death, yet another. As in every other stage, the patient may work through the period of denial quickly or in rare cases, may linger in it until the actual death. An inability to progress through any stage is seen as a signal for intervention of a counselor or doctor.[2]

The second stage, which follows denial, is that of anger. The patient feels victimized and responds, "Why did this happen to me." Or guilty, "This happened to me because . . ." Of these feelings of victimization or guilt, Dr. Kübler-Ross observes that the patient often displaces their anger onto the hospital staff, the doctor, or even the patient's family—who tend to respond in kind, unless made aware of the real cause of attack—envy of good health.[3]

"If we have been unable to face the sad facts in the first period and have been angry at people and God in the second phase, maybe we can succeed in entering into some sort of agreement which may postpone the inevitable happening."[4] Dr. Kübler-Ross has observed this behavior in her patients and calls it the bargaining stage. She notes that the patient "knows from past experiences, that there is a slim chance that he may be rewarded for good behavior and be granted a wish for special services. His wish is most always an extension of life followed by the wish for a few days without pain or physical discomfort . . . The bargaining is really an attempt to postpone; it has to include a prize offered 'for good behavior,' it also sets a self-imposed 'deadline' (e.g. one more performance [attending] the son's wedding), and it includes an implicit promise that the patient will not ask for more if this one postponement is granted."[5] This promise, however, is never kept. If the desired wish is granted, another replaces it. Often the bargains are made with God and offer "a life dedicated to God" or "a life in the service of the church" in exchange for some additional time."[6]

In the fourth stage, depression, the patient who has admitted their illness, resented it, and bargained for health, becomes filled with a sense of great loss because of increased physical discomfort and financial burden.[7] The depression may be divided into two types—reactive and preparatory. The reactive depression results from the patient's apprehension that they

---

2. Kübler-Ross, *On Death and Dying*, 38–42.
3. Kübler-Ross, *On Death and Dying*, 50–52.
4. Kübler-Ross, *On Death and Dying*, 82.
5. Kübler-Ross, *On Death and Dying*, 82–84.
6. Kübler-Ross, *On Death and Dying*, 84.
7. Kübler-Ross, *On Death and Dying*, 85.

are no longer able to provide for their family or pay their bills, etc. The preparatory depression stems from the necessity for the patient to grieve for their lost life and is seen by Kübler-Ross as necessary to reaching a stage of acceptance.

Hope, whether it is in the world to come, or the drug to come, or the sudden miraculous exception to all rules remission to come, is common to all patients and all stages. Only in the terminal stage is there evidence that hope is lost.[8]

Finally, after these stages have been worked through, there comes a time when the terminally ill accept their illness and experience some peace with themselves. After this acceptance of themselves and of their own dying, they are able to die peacefully. When many people reach this stage of acceptance, they then enter a terminal stage in which they cut themselves off from their friends, family, and hospital staff until they do not maintain human relationships anymore and finally die.[9]

---

8. Kübler-Ross, *On Death and Dying*, 76.
9. Kübler-Ross, *On Death and Dying*, 112–37.

Value of Kübler-Ross Study

After describing these stages, Dr. Kübler-Ross includes some interviews with the terminally ill, which demonstrate the dynamics used by the individual patient in coping with their emotions. In conclusion, she re-emphasizes the value of the study. The consecutive emotional stages experienced by terminally ill patients have been defined and various coping mechanisms used by these patients have been discussed. The patient's need for empathetic relationships, both with staff and family members, during this entire period is stressed. An increase in the number of these relationships has been observed as a result of the heightened awareness of the staff following the study. They have ranged from an improved doctor-patient and nurse-patient relationship, to the sharing of problems by patients hospitalized with the same disease, either through group therapy or a "buddy system" outpatient support-group; in addition to the overt benefit experienced by the patient through the recognition of and the response to their emotional needs, those professionals who were involved in the study gained an increased understanding of their own feelings about death and dying through their relationships with the patients. The entire experience speaks strongly to the therapeutic role of empathetic relationships and points out the need for human beings to maintain such relationships.

Donne's Emotional States

John Donne's account of his illness strengthens the basic observations of the Kübler-Ross study through an identification of similar feelings experienced in another time and culture. In large part, the two works are complementary. Donne, too, passes through stages of shock, anger, loneliness, and depression before he achieves acceptance. He, too, exhibits coping mechanisms drawn from his life script. He, too, needs to communicate his feelings to others and gains strength from sharing the suffering of his dying neighbor. He does not experience a separate stage of denial, although this technique is used in coping with his apprehension over the doctor's actions. Neither does he engage in specific bargaining. His overt expression of fear of the doctor's treatment, however, is far more direct than that found in patients of Dr. Kübler-Ross, a difference which probably reflects a more tolerant cultural acceptance of fear in the seventeenth century than is present today. Certainly, Donne's work, as that of Kübler-Ross, is valuable as a teaching instrument for understanding the dynamics of the emotional stages of the seriously ill.

DIFFUSE ANXIETY

Just as in the patients that Kübler-Ross talked with, Donne's initial reaction to his sudden illness was one of shock. His first meditation expresses this state, in which he voices both explicitly and implicitly the anxiety that he is experiencing and will continue to experience until the acceptance stage. The exclamations with which he begins each section of this meditation express the distress that he is experiencing. "Variable, and therfore miserable condition of Man; this minute I was well, and am ill, this minute" introduces his dislike of his changed state, of which he had no warning and for which he was unprepared.[10] The second misery—"O miserable condition of Man, which was not imprinted by *God*, who . . . is *immortall* himselfe" cries out against the fact that we are subject to and must all experience that final change—death;[11] while the third cry of misery "O multiplied misery! we die, and cannot enjoy death, because wee die in this torment of sicknes"[12] expresses distress that man experiences sickness. Finally, the meditation closes with three lamentations over the situation. "O perplex'd discomposition, O ridling distemper, O miserable condition of Man."[13]

In addition to Donne's lamentations, his choice of images for his illness is an indication of how he views his situation. His sickness is a cannon that has destroyed his carefully built and maintained health. "We study *Health*, and we deliberate upon our *meats*, and *drink*, and *ayre*, and *exercises*, and we hew, and wee polish every stone, that goes to that building; and so our *Health* is a long and a regular work; But in a minute a Canon batters all, overthrowes all, demolishes all."[14] Sickness is personified as an attacker, who despite precautions, has succeeded in a direct assault. "A *Sicknes* unprevented for all our diligence, unsuspected for all our curiositie; nay, undeserved, if we consider only *disorder*, summons us, seizes us, possesses us, destroyes us in an instant."[15] The images of violence continue as Donne next calls sickness an instrument of torture. "We doe not onely die, but die upon the Rack, die by the torment of sicknesse."[16] He moves now to compare his illness to violence in nature—earthquakes, lightning, thunder, eclipses, shooting stars, and rivers of blood. "Is this the honour which Man hath by being

10. Donne, *Devotions* (Sparrow), 1.
11. Donne, *Devotions* (Sparrow), 1.
12. Donne, *Devotions* (Sparrow), 1.
13. Donne, *Devotions* (Sparrow), 2.
14. Donne, *Devotions* (Sparrow), 1.
15. Donne, *Devotions* (Sparrow), 1.
16. Donne, *Devotions* (Sparrow), 1.

a *little world*, That he hath these *earthquakes* in him selfe, sodaine shakings; these *lightnings*, sodaine flashes; these *thunders*, sodaine noises; these *Eclypses*, sodain offuscations, and darknings of his senses; these *Blazing stars*, sodaine fiery exhalations; these *Rivers of blood*, sodaine red waters?"[17]

If the distress that Donne feels over his illness is expressed in his use of exclamatory language and his choice of violent imagery, it is also directly presented in his description of the uncontrollable anxiety that he feels. "We are tormented with sicknes, and cannot stay till the torment come, but pre-apprehensions and presages, prophecy those torments, which induce that *death* before either come; and our dissolution is conceived in these *first changes*, *quickned* in the *sicknes* it selfe, and *borne* in *death*, which beares date from these first changes."[18] It is an anxiety which he feels to be self-destructive to his possible recovery, but he is unable to allay:

> Is he a *world* to himselfe onely therefore, that he hath inough in himself, not only to destroy, and execute himselfe, but to presage that execution upon himselfe; to assist the sicknes, to antidate the sicknes, to make the sicknes the more irremediable, by sad apprehensions, and as if he would make a fire the more vehement, by sprinkling water upon the coales, so to wrap a hote fever in cold Melancholy, least the fever alone should not destroy fast enough, without this contribution, nor perfit the work (which is *destruction*) except we joynd an artificiall sicknes, of our owne *melancholy*, to our natural, our unnaturall fever.[19]

Donne is, then, experiencing diffuse anxiety over an illness which he perceives as threatening to his ability to control his life, as well as to his life itself.

Absence of Denial

Following the initial reaction of shock to the illness, Kübler-Ross notes a period of denial in many patients. "Denial functions as a buffer after unexpected shocking news, allows the patient to collect himself and, with time, mobilize other, less radical defenses."[20] Denial as a stage is, however, absent from Donne's stages of adjustment. Perhaps this is because he suffers from an illness from which he knows he *may* die, rather than from an illness from which he is told definitely that he *will* die. Although he consistently

---

17. Donne, *Devotions* (Sparrow), 2.
18. Donne, *Devotions* (Sparrow), 1–2.
19. Donne, *Devotions* (Sparrow), 2.
20. Kübler-Ross, *On Death and Dying*, 39.

contemplates the event of his own death, he continues to maintain some hope that somehow, he will survive. This maintenance of hope is also observed by Kübler-Ross, but due to the finality of the diagnosis, it has a slightly different expression—hope in the discovery of a cure, in a remission, in a misdiagnosis, in a miracle. Donne does, however, use denial as a coping mechanism during his illness. The section in which he closely follows the actions of the physician, his decision to consult, to prescribe, and pursue a course of treatment, contains the implied denial of the thought that the disease is fatal, no matter what is done. He consistently denies that he fears death, also. "I feare not the hastening of my *death*, and yet I do fear the increase of the *disease*; I should belie Nature, if I should deny that I feared this, and if I should say that I feared *death*, I should belye *God*."[21] To admit fear of death is to admit that there is something wrong with his relationship with God, an admission that is too threatening to deal with directly. Therefore, Donne continues to maintain this posture until, in his acceptance of his humanity, he achieves that relationship with God which permits him to truly accept his own death and not to fear.

With the exception of his denial of a fear of death, however, Donne does not use denial even as a coping device as consistently as the twentieth-century patients. This may be related to the different types of danger that twentieth-century patients live under. Kübler-Ross observes that "in the old days, a man was able to face his enemy eye to eye. He had a fair chance in a personal encounter with a visible enemy. Now the soldier as well as the civilian has to anticipate weapons of mass destruction which offer no one a reasonable chance, often not even an awareness of their approach. Destruction can strike out of the blue skies and destroy thousands like the bomb at Hiroshima; it may come in the form of gases or other means of chemical warfare—invisible, crippling, killing."[22] Faced with ever imminent impersonal destruction, man has adapted by denying that this capability is present. This denial is also used when presented with climate change, overpopulation, mass poverty, and possible famine. Our age is one of overwhelming problems that the individual feels powerless to change and so shuts out. Once this technique is learned, it is applied to those things that we could control such as the destruction of health by alcohol and drug abuse.

The world of John Donne, however, did not present these impersonal threats. There, the dangers could be defined and fought against. It is not that seventeenth-century Englishmen lived without the threat of danger. Rather, it was a danger with which one still had the feeling he could cope. Political

21. Donne, *Devotions* (Sparrow), 28–29.
22. Kübler-Ross, *On Death and Dying*, 12.

and religious intrigue and persecution were the rule, and violence was often encountered in affairs of state. It was obviously more dangerous, however, to deny the existence of these threats, than to acknowledge them, because retribution was swift and few men escaped by ignoring the presence of the threat, whether it was pestilence, or political enemies, or personal vendetta. It would seem logical, then, for Donne not to employ this defense mechanism as extensively as we do today. In line with this seventeenth-century tendency to seek to allay problems through direct confrontation, Donne spends his second meditation defining exactly what his illness is rather than denying it.

Another characteristic of the late-sixteenth and early-seventeenth century England was man's image of himself as an independent and self-sufficient being. This self-reliant image was a result of Renaissance humanism, which glorified man's innate capabilities. The unity of the Roman Catholic church had been destroyed by the Reformation, and feudalism had been replaced by the rise of national power. Men, although no longer secure in religious unity and feudal protection, identified with the new power of their country and developed their own powers in art, literature, science, and philosophy. The exhilaration of the sixteenth-century Renaissance, however, gave way to feelings of isolation in the seventeenth century.

Without the support of church and guild, man not only was able to act independently, he *had* to. The seventeenth century, then, continued to work on the problems of independence, after the initial euphoria over the achievement of independence was gone.[23] Self-reliance was a natural concern of Donne and loss of it carried a big threat. This is apparent in the frustration he expresses over its loss in Meditations III–V.

Anger

Kübler-Ross has observed that "when the first stage of denial cannot be maintained any longer, it is replaced by feelings of anger, rage, envy, and resentment."[24] Donne follows this same pattern in Meditations III–V in which he is obviously venting his anger as he protests against being in bed, having to call a doctor, and being alone. Instead of saying that he is angry at being critically ill, he complains at length about the conditions attendant on that illness. For a lengthy explication of the passages see Part One. Once again, the feeling tone of the passages, and the choice of images, as well as the direct statement of dislike for his situation, indicates his frustration

---

23. Fromm, *Escape from Freedom*, 56–122.
24. Kübler-Ross, *On Death and Dying*, 50.

at losing his independence. "Miserable and, (though common to all) inhuman *posture*, where I must practise my lying in the *grave*, by lying still, and not practise my *Resurrection*, by rising any more."[25] The sick bed is called a prison, in which weakness of muscle is an effective manacle. "Strange fetters to the feete, strange Manacles to the hands, when the feete, and handes are bound so much the faster, by how much the coards are slacker; So much the lesse able to doe their Offices, by how much more the Sinewes and Ligaments are the looser."[26] "I . . . am in a close prison, in a sicke bed."[27] He also sees his sick bed as a grave. "A sicke bed, is a grave; and all that the patient saies there, is but a varying of his owne *Epitaph*."[28] Indeed the solitude of illness makes his confinement worse than that of a grave: "As the height of an infectious disease of the body, is *solitude*, to be left alone: for this makes an infectious bed, equall, nay worse than a grave, that thogh in both I be equally alone, in my bed I *know* it, and *feele* it, and shall not in my *grave*: and this too, that in my bedd, my soule is still in an infectious body, and shall not in my grave bee so."[29]

The loss of independence of movement is seen as inhuman. "Wee attribute but one priviledge and advantage to Mans body, above other moving creatures, that he is not as others, groveling, but of an erect, of an upright form, naturally built, and disposed to the contemplation of *Heaven*."[30] The dependence on a physician indicates a lack of a self–sufficiency that even animals have: "Man hath not that *innate instinct*, to apply these naturall medicines to his present danger, as those inferiour creatures have; he is not his owne *Apothecary*, his owne *Phisician*, as they are . . . whats become of mans great extent and proportion, when himselfe shrinkes himselfe, and consumes himselfe to a handfull of dust; whats become of his soaring thoughts, his compassing thoughts, when himselfe brings himselfe to the ignorance, to the thoughtlessnesse of the *Grave*?"[31] The loss of companionship is also seen as against the preconceived order of God. "*God* himself wold admit a *figure* of *Society*, as there is a plurality of persons in *God*, though there bee but one *God*; and all his externall actions testifie a love of *Societie*, and *communion*."[32] He concludes that "Men that inhere upon *Nature* only, are so

25. Donne, *Devotions* (Sparrow), 11.
26. Donne, *Devotions* (Sparrow), 11.
27. Donne, *Devotions* (Sparrow), 16.
28. Donne, *Devotions* (Sparrow), 11.
29. Donne, *Devotions* (Sparrow), 24.
30. Donne, *Devotions* (Sparrow), 10.
31. Donne, *Devotions* (Sparrow), 17.
32. Donne, *Devotions* (Sparrow), 23.

far from thinking, that there is anything *singular* in this world, as that they will scarce thinke, that this world it selfe is *singular*, but that every *Planet*, and every *Starre*, is another *world* like this; They finde reason to conceive, not onely a *pluralitie* in every *Species* in the world, but a *pluralitie of worlds*; so that the abhorrers of *Solitude*, are not solitary; for *God*, and *Nature*, and *Reason* concurre against it."[33]

Thus, Donne feels that being bedridden is an inhuman posture, being dependent on the doctor is worse than animal behavior, and that being alone is ungodlike, inhuman, and unnatural. Disease itself is seen as monster-like:

> And then as the other *world* produces *Serpents*, and *Vipers*, malignant, and venimous creatures, and *Wormes*, and *Caterpillars*, that endeavour to devour that world which produces them, and *Monsters* compiled and complicated of divers parents, and kinds, so this world, our selves, produces all these in us, in producing *diseases*, and *sicknesses*, of all those sorts; venimous, and infectious diseases, feeding and consuming diseases, and manifold and entangled diseases, made up of many several ones. And can the other world name so many *venimous*, so many consuming, so many monstrous creatures, as we can diseases, of all these kindes?[34]

And his first reference to the doctor is as a superhuman champion against these monsters.

Fear

In Meditations III–V, Donne is verbalizing feelings of impotency which his changed situation has aroused. He has physically experienced a loss of independence. He has lost his normal ability to care for himself. His illness has separated him from other people, it has made him unable to move around, and has confined him to a bed where he lies too weak to feed himself or to even change his position. Furthermore, he realizes that he does not have the ability to cure himself, that he must depend on a doctor. This increases his feelings of inadequacy. He expresses his distress over his changed condition, and his inability to act in it through anger at having to go to bed, to depend on the doctor, and to be alone—specific things which irritate him. In the next section, Meditations VI–X, Donne copes with the underlying impotency that he is feeling by concentrating on the management of his illness. Anxiety

---

33. Donne, *Devotions* (Sparrow), 23–24.
34. Donne, *Devotions* (Sparrow), 16–17.

which was expressed as anger at this situation has been superseded by feelings of fear for his life, which are not directly expressed, but worked through one step removed with the discussion of his concern over the doctor's actions. Throughout this section there is great emphasis on fear. The doctor is afraid of the outcome of the disease. Donne is afraid because the doctor is afraid and tries to hide this fear. He verbalizes that he is afraid of the increase of his illness and the outcome of the disease. He denies that he is afraid of his death. He analyzes the different ways that fear may be exhibited, and the irrational fears that a man may feel. He asserts what fear can and cannot do. Following this first meditation in which Donne speaks openly of his own fear over the increase of the disease, but stops short of verbalizing his fear of death, are three meditations in which he expresses his anxiety over the outcome of his illness, through his obsessive concern over the doctor's actions. In Meditation VII, the doctor, who has been unable to make a diagnosis, calls in other doctors as consultants. Donne interprets this action to indicate that the disease has advanced. This is such a threatening idea that he immediately looks for other reasons for having consults—for example: this shows the doctor is careful and not personally ambitious; or, it is not necessarily an indication of advancing illness to have consults; and it certainly does not increase the danger. Rather, more doctors bring to bear more knowledge on the diagnosis and that is good. Then, he digresses on the subject of doctors, and their aid in general, pointing out that many people are sick and do not have physicians, or a place to stay, or medicine. At this point he closes, noting that he is thankful for his doctors. This closure is tangential to the original question—i.e. does the fact that the doctor needs to consult mean that the illness is worse? And to the original assumption that he expresses—"if the *Phisician* desire help, the burden grows great: There is a growth of the *Disease* then"[35]—but this original assumption does not express his belief that he shall die from this disease.

In Meditation IX, Donne is still following the doctors' actions, closely examining them for any adverse indications, and speedily thinking of alternative explanations, if those adverse indications seem to appear. The other doctors have been consulted, among them the king's own physician, and they are conferring over what to do. "They have seene me, and heard mee, arraign'd mee in these fetters, and receiv'd the *evidence*; I have cut up mine *Anatomy*, dissected my selfe, and they are gon to *read* upon me."[36] He is depressed by the very number of possible sicknesses there are:

> There are more *sicknesses* then *names*. If *ruine* were reduc'd to
> that one way, that Man could perish noway but by *sicknes*, yet his

---

35. Donne, *Devotions* (Sparrow), 35.
36. Donne, *Devotions* (Sparrow), 48.

danger were infinit; and if *sicknes* were reduc'd to that one way, that there were no *sicknes* but a *fever*, yet the way were infinite still; it would overlode, and oppress any naturall, disorder and discompose any artificiall *Memory*, to deliver the *names* of severall *fevers*; how intricate a worke then have they, who are gone to *consult*, which of these *sicknesses* mine is, and then which of these *fevers*, and then what it would do, and then how it may be countermind.[37]

He does not dwell on the difficulty of making a diagnosis, however; instead, he continues to give reasons why consultation itself is a good sign. It means that he is not in immediate danger if there is time to deliberate. This conclusion is illustrated by examples of physical and mental illness and of civil disorders that would not wait for consultation due to their gravity. He then states once again that he is glad there is time for consultations and writing prescriptions. And again, he gives examples of events which call for immediate action. And then, once more, he states that he is glad the doctors consult, prescribe, and prescribe medicine, and expresses thankfulness that they do not admonish him for what he did not do or tell him what to do later—that they confine their treatment to the present. Finally, for the fourth time, he says he is "glad they know (I have hid nothing from them) glad they consult, (they hide nothing from one another) glad they write (they hide nothing from the world) glad that they write and prescribe *Phisick*, that there are *remedies* for the present case."[38] His reiteration of thankfulness over each action of the physician has become a litany, ritualistically used to keep off bad luck, to reassure himself that what is done is all right. But the assurance is hollow, coming as it does after Donne's pessimistic appraisal of the difficulty of correct diagnosis. The mood swings signal his underlying anxiety; which comes out more directly in Meditation X, when he realizes that the treatment has not resulted in the hoped–for cure. "They find the Disease to steale on insensibly, and endeavour to meet with it so."[39] They have not halted its course for all of Donne's ritual, "they see, that invisibly, and I feele, that insensibly the *disease* prevailes,"[40] and although Donne voices some optimism that against the insensible disease "*Phisicians* have their *examiners*; and those these employ now,"[41] this is his last attempt to find favorable signs in the doctors' actions.

37. Donne, *Devotions* (Sparrow), 48–49.
38. Donne, *Devotions* (Sparrow), 50.
39. Donne, *Devotions* (Sparrow), 54.
40. Donne, *Devotions* (Sparrow), 56.
41. Donne, *Devotions* (Sparrow), 56.

There is no section in Kübler-Ross's stages that is comparable to this expression of fear over the outcome of his illness that Donne shows in these meditations. There is obviously denial operating in his choosing to concentrate on the day-to-day actions of the doctor and not going on to look at the implications of the illness. The ritualistic reiteration of assurances that the doctor is doing the right thing may even be seen as a form of bargaining for health by agreeing to follow directions. The principal emotion, however, remains that of fear—fear expressed both overtly and covertly, as verbalized fear of the advance of the illness and the doctors' treatment of it through which Donne is able to localize and manage his diffuse anxiety over the possibility of death. He is able to speak freely of the doctor's fear and of his own in response to that fear. He unashamedly allows himself to acknowledge that he is afraid of the illness and its prognosis. He only denies the fear of death, because that would threaten his stated belief in God.

Kübler-Ross has observed that "death is still a fearful, frightening happening, and the fear of death is a universal fear even if we think we have mastered it on many levels. What has changed is our way of coping and dealing with death and dying and our dying patients."[42] Why has the overt expression of fear diminished as a stage in the dying process? Perhaps the first reason might be that our culture no longer allows the expression of fear. We have lived in an age of positive thinking, still dominated by lip service to the idea of progress despite the adverse evidence of two world wars and atomic weapons, where to mention possible lack of national growth, or personal achievement, or security, is to be labeled a misanthrope, a pessimist who is out of step with a progressive world. We are still adhering to the ancient belief that to name a thing, is to call it into being. Certainly, we do not want to conjure up thermonuclear war, or famine, or disease. If we do not mention these things, neither do we mention our fear of them. Denial creates denial and repression, repression. Thus, it is natural for patients to not speak readily of their fear and to ventilate their anxiety in less direct mechanisms. Patients do describe to the staff that they are worried about different things—the misdiagnoses of disease, the mismanagement of the nursing staff, the loss of their jobs. Their anxiety remains, even if there is more hesitancy to label this anxiety as fear. In the description of an experience of a chaplain who had thought he had a malignancy, this stage of diffuse anxiety is mentioned: "He had developed enlarged lymph glands and was asked to have a biopsy taken in order to evaluate the possibility of a malignancy. He attended the next seminar and shared with the group the stages of shock, dismay, and disbelief he had gone through—the days

---

42. Kübler-Ross, *On Death and Dying*, 5.

of anger, depression, and hope, alternating with utter anxiety and fear."[43] Perhaps, then, we have in Donne's experience one of those times in which fear overwhelms the patient. It is such a definite period, however, that it will be labeled as a separate stage. A second reason why no stage of overt fear has been found in Dr. Kübler-Ross's patients may be that this is a very private experience and Donne may have felt more freedom to communicate this feeling in his writing than people would feel when verbally expressing it.

Depression

Beginning with Meditation XI, Donne enters the stage best described as depression. His observations of the treatment chosen by the doctors no longer end in optimistic summaries. Rather, he is depressed by the enormity of the undertaking. The total dependence of life on the continuation of the function of the heart is noted in Meditation XI. "How little of a *Man* is the *Heart*, and yet it is all, by which he *is*; and this continually subject, not only to forraine poysons, conveyed by others, but to intestine poysons, bred in ourselves by pestilentiall sicknesses."[44] He is depressed also because the doctors tell him that his anxiety, his melancholy is causing vapors which are detrimental to his recovery. "But what have I done, either to *breed*, or to *breath* these *vapors*? They tell me it is my *Melancholy*; Did I infuse, did I drinke in *Melancholly* into my selfe? . . . It is my *study*; doth not my *Calling* call for that? I have don nothing, wilfully, perversely toward it, yet must suffer in it, die by it."[45] Here Donne cries out against the unjustness of his situation. "I doe nothing upon my selfe, and yet am mine owne *Executioner*."[46] He is angry once more, but the anger subsides into his depression again when he is informed that he has a pestilential illness. Instead of thinking of all the advantages there are to establishing a diagnosis, Donne uses the identification of his illness to feed his depression. "That an enemy *declares* himselfe, then, when he is able to subsist, and to pursue, and to atchive his ends, is no great comfort . . . It is a faint comfort to know the worst, when the worst is *remedilesse*; and a weaker than that, to know *much ill*, and not to know, that that is the worst."[47] He no longer attempts to cope by citing analogies or examples. The ones he does use help to feed his distress rather than alleviate it. Throughout this stage, external events make Donne aware

43. Kübler-Ross, *On Death and Dying*, 255.
44. Donne, *Devotions* (Sparrow), 63.
45. Donne, *Devotions* (Sparrow), 69.
46. Donne, *Devotions* (Sparrow), 69.
47. Donne, *Devotions* (Sparrow), 74–75.

of his own impotence. He has no control over his physical condition as exemplified in his heart, or over his emotions, as exemplified in the vapors caused by melancholia. His disease, which is finally identified as severe, but without remedy, has reached the time of critical days which are also out of Donne's control. His anxiety and depression culminate in a state of agitated depression. He wants to sleep to get away from his troubles and yet does not have the ability to even induce sleep.

Obviously, this rather classic description of a depression is comparable to the depressed state that Kübler-Ross noticed in her patients: "When the terminally ill patient can no longer deny his illness, when he is forced to undergo more surgery or hospitalization, when he begins to have more symptoms or becomes weaker and thinner, he cannot smile it off anymore. His numbness or stoicism, his anger and rage will soon be replaced with a sense of great loss."[48] Kübler-Ross stresses the difference between a depression over loss of activities, which may be coped with, and a depression over loss of life itself, which is part of that grieving that is experienced in preparation for the acceptance stage. Donne's depression, however, is in response to his loss of independence, his loss of control over his life. He does not grieve over the loss of his body until when, in Meditation XVIII, he grieves vicariously over the loss of the other man's body. This difference in depression is probably due to the fact that Donne is not directly confronted with certain death. Rather, he is reacting to his changed condition, his sick state, in which he is painfully aware of his own impotency and no longer tries to cope with this awareness. Thus, although Kübler-Ross' patients and Donne both experience depression prior to acceptance, the cause of the depression is different. Donne's depression is another particular manifestation of his generalized anxiety over his changed condition which has resulted in a loss of independence and ability to control his life. This is in line with the type of life he had led prior to illness, in which he had been successful by exhibiting just those skills and defense mechanisms of which he is no longer capable.

Kübler-Ross has observed that "earlier conflicts and defense mechanisms allow us to predict to a certain degree what defense mechanisms a patient will use more extensively at the time of crisis."[49] It appears that "people who have gone through a life of suffering, hard work, and labor, who have raised their children and been gratified in their work, have shown greater ease in accepting death with peace and dignity compared to those who have been ambitiously controlling their environment, accumulating material goods, and a great number of social relationships but few interpersonal

---

48. Kübler-Ross, *On Death and Dying*, 85.
49. Kübler-Ross, *On Death and Dying*, 265.

relationships which would have been available at the end of life."[50] She gives the example of a successful businessman who "had always been a tyrant and kept strict control over his business and his home life" who was angry over his loss of control in the hospital environment and who improved when given control over limited decisions once more.[51]

Although Donne was certainly not a stereotype of the rich, successful, organization man, he, too, was ambitious; he, too, enjoyed success in his profession; and he, too, was used to maintaining control over his environment. This personality type will be analyzed in depth in Chapter 7, but it is important to note here that Donne had spent much of his early life surviving in a hostile environment. He was an English Roman Catholic when this meant exclusion from public office and university education, persecution, and possible death.[52] He married without his wife's father's consent and in addition to incurring his displeasure (Donne lost his job and was imprisoned), Donne suffered years of penury because of this action. He had a real, as well as a psychological, need to feel in control of his life which had been so vulnerable to external events and when he took orders and rose in the church, he thrived on his success. Thus, when the sudden change of illness underscored his inability to control his situation, he reacted with anger at the loss, with fear over his unprotected situation, and with despair over his impotency. And so, the dependencies attendant upon a debilitating illness take on an exaggerated threat to Donne, whose self-reliance was built on a low trust level of others which did not allow for close personal friendships.

Acceptance and Hope

After experiencing depression over his impotency to alter his illness, Donne reaches an acceptance of his situation in Meditations XVI–XVIII. The passing bell makes him aware of the commonality of suffering and he finds comfort in sharing this suffering. As he asserts "No man is an *Iland*, intire of it selfe . . . any mans *death* diminishes *me*, because I am involved in *Mankinde*; And therefore never send to know for whom the *bell* tolls; It tolls for *thee*," he has made a major shift in his orientation.[53] No longer striving to be independent, he feels a part of humanity and accepts his situation. He no longer attempts to control his life and with his acceptance, he is free of his consuming self-concern and able to participate in the concerns of other

---

50. Kübler-Ross, *On Death and Dying*, 265.
51. Kübler-Ross, *On Death and Dying*, 55.
52. Hunt, *Donne's Poetry*, 170.
53. Donne, *Devotions* (Sparrow), 98.

humans. A detailed analysis of this acceptance has been given earlier. It will be discussed here in relationship to the acceptance reached by the dying patients that Kübler-Ross saw.

Once again, although the phenomenon is the same, the expression it takes is different, again in direct relationship to the nature of the change that has been resisted. Kübler-Ross's patients have largely been involved with a struggle against the change of their death and when they reach an acceptance of that death, they are usually physically dying and now are psychologically adjusted to that physical change. Donne, although overtly adjusting to a critical illness, has primarily been working through the anxiety felt by a sudden change that makes him aware of his loss of control, his impotency. He has expressed that anxiety in terms of anger, loneliness, fear, and depression; first fighting against his situation and then feeling depressed by it before he reaches a psychological acceptance of his physical condition. In either situation, the psychological acceptance of a changed physical condition comes only after experiencing and working through various psychological stages. Kübler-Ross calls those "defense mechanisms to deal with the extremely difficult situations" and asserts that "the one thing that usually persists through all these stages is hope."[54] Her patients maintain hope in a cure, a remission, a new medicine, and react against having that hope squelched.

Donne also expresses hope throughout the course of his illness. At the same time that he is objecting to needing the help of a doctor, he sees him as a superhuman aid against disease. "But wee have a *Hercules* against these *Gyants*, these *Monsters*; that is, the *Phisician*; hee musters up al the forces of the other world, to succour this; all Nature to relieve Man."[55] Throughout the state of fear, he expresses hope in the physicians' ability. "My *Phisicians* fear puts not him from his *practise*."[56] He keeps his spirits up by arguments that consultations with other doctors means that his doctor is more thorough, that more consults equal more aids to fight disease, and that time for consultation means that the disease is not immediately critical. Even when the disease continues to advance, he keeps up his hopes by saying he is glad that he has a physician to work on determining the cause of the illness.

Although hope is obviously less present in his depression, it still appears as a coping mechanism. When spots appear, he tells himself that they help the doctors establish a diagnosis and they will then know better what to do "if there be a *comfort* in the declaration, that therby the *Phisicians* see

---

54. Kübler-Ross, *On Death and Dying*, 138.
55. Donne, *Devotions* (Sparrow), 17.
56. Donne, *Devotions* (Sparrow), 29.

more cleerely what to doe."[57] Again, when the physicians apply pigeons, Donne verbalizes his hope that the treatment will work. "Be a good *Pigeon* to draw this *vapor* from the Head, and from doing any deadly harme there."[58]

After his acceptance of his illness, Meditation XIX is filled with hope. Everything is seen in a good light. He sees the time itself as ripe for an improvement in the illness: "All this while the *Physitians* themselves have beene *patients*, patiently attending when they should see any *land* in this *Sea*, any *earth*, any *cloud*, any *indication* of *concoction* in these *waters* . . . they must stay till the *season* of the sicknesse come, and till it be ripened of it selfe, and then they may put to their hand, to *gather* it before it *fall* off, but they cannot hasten the *ripening*."[59] It would be unnatural for the doctors to cure before the disease was at the right stage. "Why should wee looke for that in *disorder*, in a *disease*, when we cannot have it in Nature, who is so *regular*, and so *pregnant*, so forward to bring her worke to perfection, and to light? Yet we cannot awake the *July-flowers* in *January*, nor retard the *flowers* of the *spring* to *autumne*."[60] He has, then, explained why it has taken so long for the physician's cure to work. The choice of images—flowers, fruit, birth—are expectant, positive, happy images. The earlier meditation, XVI, which deals with critical days has none of this optimism. There, critical days are fatalistically seen as one more evidence of Donne's impotency. Now, however, he is in accord with nature and the wholeness of his unity is affirmed in the positive way that he views times and seasons. He also trusts the physicians now, compares them to sentinels who watch for a change of conditions, calling their cordials munitions. He feels in himself a rallying that will allow him to "*fight*, and so die in the *field*," not die "in a prison."[61] The entire meditation has a sense of openness and resolution that has been absent until this time. Renewed hope is the essence of the section.

---

57. Donne, *Devotions* (Sparrow), 74.
58. Donne, *Devotions* (Sparrow), 70.
59. Donne, *Devotions* (Sparrow), 110–11.
60. Donne, *Devotions* (Sparrow), 111.
61. Donne, *Devotions* (Sparrow), 112.

Summary

Thus, John Donne uses many of the same coping mechanisms in his emotional adjustment to sudden critical illness that Kübler-Ross has observed in her study of behavior of the terminally ill. Diffuse anxiety, anger, loneliness, fear, depression, and hope are directly observed and indirectly expressed in the *Devotions upon Emergent Occasions* by means of imagery and choice of language. It has been demonstrated that Donne does not use as much denial as twentieth-century patients and that his expression of fear is much more direct. This difference may be related to the frequency with which those coping mechanisms occurred in a particular age. The general similarity of the pattern of adjustment under stress found in Donne and the Kübler-Ross study, despite a difference of three hundred and fifty years and a vast shift in cultural values, attests to the basic universality of the psychological phenomena experienced. Although conditioned by the age in which it occurs, the psychological responses are not created by a specific environment but are ways of coping with the physiological anxiety response that occurs whenever sudden, undesired change occurs or is anticipated. This anxiety is, then, a normal response to a perceived threat, and it is natural and necessary for men to use various means of expressing that anxiety—anger, depression—while adjusting to a changed state.

The basic psychological problem in *Devotions upon Emergent Occasions* is the problem of how a person handles change—more specifically, abrupt change—in his or her life style. In the fifty-first year of his life, John Donne—poet, writer, scholar, theologian, and successful cleric—is struck down with an unknown illness. Although he is overwhelmed at first with anxiety, and expresses both anger over his perceived victimization and melancholia over his projected prognosis, he soon manages to define the area of his concern and to proceed to work on his feelings within those limits. After concentrating on the new living conditions which his illness imposes on him, he focuses on the behavior of the doctors as the disease progresses. His anxiety during this period is expressed in two different ways. First, he analyzes the doctors' actions, expresses concern over their efficacy, and produces reasons to hope for a good prognosis. Then, as he continues to grow worse, he comments on the doctors' actions, but without any expression of optimism. This melancholia deepens, and Donne experiences agitated depression. He sees his illness as a reality which he is unable to alter, but against which he continues to fight. Finally, after being reminded of other men's suffering through the tolling of the passing bell, he accepts his new situation and stops trying to return to his old lifestyle. After this acceptance, he is able to function within the new environment and to fight against the disease without the great need to reject his sick state.

When he is faced with a change to well behavior, however, he once more experiences anxiety over a return to the old state, to which he is no longer adjusted. Again, he focuses this anxiety, expressing anger over the doctors' treatment, depression over his own inability to be self-sufficient, and fear over assuming the responsibility for a future relapse. Thus, we are shown two examples of one man's reaction to change. The first change, an unanticipated and undesired critical illness, is totally unexpected and Donne's adjustment to it occurs after the event has taken place; while the change from being sick to normal health is hopefully anticipated and an adjustment may take place gradually. This adjustment is, however, not without pain and similar coping devices are used for both adaptations.

The work, then, is not only presenting the progression of emotional responses that occur when a person is faced with imminent death, although that phenomenon is thoroughly exposed. Rather, by a repetition of these feelings when Donne anticipates a change for the better, it displays and emphasizes that these emotions are experienced in some degree *whenever* a change occurs or is anticipated. Although the amount of stress behavior varies with the perceived severity of the change, it is present even when the change has been looked forward to and has been expressly desired. Given this phenomenon, certain conclusions may be drawn:

1. Donne does not physically change his environment without psychologically experiencing an emotional response to that change (anxiety).

2. An emotional response is to be anticipated whenever change, whether anticipated or unexpected, occurs.

3. There are various defined emotional stages that Donne experiences in working through this generalized anxiety which occurs in response to change. These may include anger, fear, depression, and hope.

4. Within these stages, he employs with varying degrees of success, mechanisms—specifically intellectualizations, analogies, extended scientific and religious analyzations, and prayers—in an attempt to control the particular manifestation of anxiety with which he is dealing.

5. Despite Donne's efforts to "control" these different manifestations of anxiety, they continue to appear in new ways until such time as he can accept his changed status.

His coping behavior, then, offers immediate relief, but does not solve the underlying cause of his expressed distress. He has himself observed the phenomenon. "In many *diseases*, that which is but an *accident*, but a *symptom* of the main *disease*, is so violent, that the *Phisician* must attend the cure of that, though hee pretermit (so far as to intermit) the cure of the *disease* it self."[62] It is only when he emotionally accepts the physical change that the basic anxiety that is behind the anger, fear, and depression is allayed.

If, indeed, the psychological states that Kübler-Ross's patients illustrate and Donne's writing describes are a necessary part of adjustment to change—in these instances the changes brought by terminal or critical illness and anticipated death—then these examples would serve to reinforce the argument of Toffler that the body has difficulty in adapting to rapid change and that much physical and mental illness may be traced to that cause, i.e. the experiencing of several major changes in rapid succession.[63] He cites examples from the work of Hinkle, Holmes, Rahe, Arthur, and McKean who have studied the relationship of change to illness. "For the first time," says Dr. Arthur, appraising life change research, "we have an index of change. If you've had many changes in your life within a short time, this places a great challenge on your body . . . An enormous number of changes within a short period might overwhelm its coping mechanisms."[64]

Certainly, the time that Donne and Kübler-Ross indicate is necessary to work through one major adjustment would reinforce these observations. Although entire books have been written on the subject of change (*Future Shock* is only one of a large body of such literature) and the subject itself is too broad to be reviewed in this work, it is interesting to note that the problems of adaptation to change have been a major theme in literature. Shakespeare points out the danger of disturbing the political order in his history plays; Thomas Hardy's characters struggle with a change in their physical environment; Chekhov's play, *The Cherry Orchard*, presents people adapting to social change; and Sophocles' *Antigone* portrays the conflict caused by a change in demanded loyalties. The confusion caused by change is also a major source of comedy, which seeks to correct any deviation from the established order by means of ridicule. Throughout this literature, there is a desire to reestablish order after a change has disrupted the old organization, and there is an inherent agreement that order is necessary for any sort of resolution of action. These master plots, then, repeated in all languages and cultures, in relation to personal life and political wellbeing, are indicative of the universally observed need of man to organize his environment and to

---

62. Donne, *Devotions* (Sparrow), 49.
63. Toffler, *Future Shock*, 561.
64. Toffler, *Future Shock*, 332.

struggle against any disorganization. Donne and Kübler-Ross present case studies that help give insight into why this strong pull toward order is present. When one sees the amount of distress that Donne experiences before he accepts his new environment, it is no wonder that men seek to avoid this experience. And yet, as Toffler states, "to eliminate ORs (orientation responses) and adaptive reactions would be to eliminate all change, including growth, self–development, maturation."[65] It is in such time of crisis that man has the most potential for rapid growth. Certainly, Donne's expansion of awareness during his adjustment to a new orientation attests to this observation. Within the broadly defined study of man's psychological adaptation to change that is John Donne's *Devotions*, there is found, in Donne's description of his relationship with his physician, an excellent delineation of that perspective with which a person undergoing a reorientation crisis views external stimuli.

---

65. Toffler, *Future Shock*, 342.

Doctor–Patient Relationship: Threat and Benefit Perception During the Course of a Critical Illness

Since I am comming to that Holy roome
    Where, with thy Quire of Saints for evermore,
I shall be made thy Musique; As I come
    I tune the Instrument here at the dore,
    And what I must doe then, thinke here before.

Whilst my Physitians by their love are growne
    Cosmographers, and I their Mapp, who lie
Flat on this bed, that by them may be showne
    That this is my South-west discoverie
    Per fretum febris, by these streights to die,

I joy, that in these straits, I see my West;
    For, though theire currants yeeld returne to none,
What shall my West hurt me? As West and East
    In all flatt Maps (and I am one) are one,
    So death doth touch the Resurrection.

Is the Pacifique Sea my home? Or are
    The Easterne riches? Is *Jerusalem*?
Anyan, and *Magellan*, and *Gibraltare*,
    All streights, and none but streights, are wayes to them,
    Whether where *Japhet* dwelt, or *Cham*, or *Sem*.

We thinke that *Paradise* and *Calvarie*,
    Christs Crosse, and *Adams* tree, stood in one place;
Looke Lord, and finde both *Adams* met in me;
    As the first *Adams* sweat surrounds my face,
    May the last *Adams* blood my soule embrace.

So, in his purple wrapp'd receive mee Lord,
> By these his thornes give me his other Crowne;
And as to others soules I preach'd thy word,
> Be this my Text, my Sermon to my owne,
> Therefore that he may raise the Lord throws down.
>> —John Donne, *Hymne to God My God, in My Sicknesse*, December 1623[66]

---

66. Grierson, *Metaphysical*, 91.

Throughout *Devotions upon Emergent Occasions*, John Donne records his psychological reactions to his physician during a critical illness. An examination of these feelings offers new insight into the complexity of the doctor–patient relationship, and shows especially the effect of the patient's fear and hope on his view of the physician and his work. Such an examination is particularly helpful in delineating the impact that a change from normal activity to a crisis situation has on an individual's perception.

When John Donne was stricken with relapsing fever in the fall of 1623, the pestilential nature of the disease precluded any visitors. "A long sicknesse will weary friends at last, but a pestilentiall sicknes averts them from the beginning."[67] The only human relationship that he describes in *Devotions upon Emergent Occasions* is his relationship with his physicians. It is, therefore, initially surprising that Donne does not mention any closeness with his doctors. As he analyzes the doctors' functions, their demeanor, their method of diagnosis and treatment, their choice of medicine, and their successes and failures, never mentioning any personal interchanges, it becomes apparent that Donne is using the doctors and their behavior as a vehicle for projecting his own feelings of anger and depression and hope over his illness, rather than seeing his relationship with them as an opportunity for interpersonal support.

The ambivalence of Donne's feelings toward the physician is apparent in his first mention of the man in Meditation IV. "The Phisician is sent for."[68] In this section, Donne is experiencing feelings of impotency because of the physical incapacitation caused by his disease. He is very ill, bedridden, bereft of friends. In this situation, he sends for the physician, whom he places in the role of a superhuman champion against disease. "But wee have a *Hercules* against these *Gyants*, these *Monsters* [diseases]; that is, the *Phisician*; hee musters up al the forces of the other world, to succour this; all Nature to relieve Man."[69] After this attribution of superhuman powers to the doctor, Donne immediately shifts and reveals his feelings of impotency, which the need for an external savior creates:

> We *have* the *Phisician*[underline], but we *are not* the *Phisician*. Heere we shrinke in our proportion, sink in our dignitie, in respect of verie meane creatures, who are *Phisicians* to themselves. The *Hart* that is pursued and wounded, they say, knowes an Herbe, which being eaten, throwes off the arrow: A strange kind of *vomit*. The *dog* that pursues it, though hee bee subject to sicknes, even *proverbially*, knowes his *grasse* that recovers him

---

67. Donne, *Devotions* (Sparrow), 23.
68. Donne, *Devotions* (Sparrow), 15.
69. Donne, *Devotions* (Sparrow), 17.

> ... Man hath not that *innate instinct*, to apply these naturall medicines to his present danger, as those inferiour creatures have; he is not his owne *Apothecary*, his owne *Phisician*, as they are. Call back therefore thy Mediation again, and bring it downe; whats become of mans great extent and proportion, when himselfe shrinkes himselfe, and consumes himselfe to a handfull of dust; whats become of his soaring thoughts, his compassing thoughts, when himselfe brings himselfe to the ignorance, to the thoughtlessnesse of the *Grave*? His *diseases* are his owne, but the *Phisician* is not; hee hath them at home, but hee must send for the *Phisician*.[70]

In this passage, Donne expresses his feelings of helplessness in being able to alleviate his own distress in terms of his dependency on the physician. The physician is seen as a reminder that he himself is not self-sufficient, and that the situation is out of Donne's personal control. Thus, two conceptions of the doctor are juxtaposed as early as the fourth meditation: first, the physician as a superhuman helper and second, the physician as a symbol of the patient's impotency. These opposing views are developed in the sections which follow.

Meditation V, which is primarily concerned with loneliness, continues the dualistic picture of the doctor in the opening headings. "Solus adest" ("He only") and "The Phisician comes."[71] The physician is the only person to break the hated separation from society and is therefore welcome. At the same time, "he only" is a reminder that no one else has come—a cause of loneliness and anger in Donne. He knows that "when the infectiousnes of the disease deterrs them who should assist, from comming; even the *Phisician* dares scarse come."[72] The loneliness and scarcity of aid has become a reminder that he has a serious illness, which evokes anxiety in Donne. This anxiety is increased as he watches the physician examine him. "The Phisician is afraid."[73]—perhaps not only over the severity of the illness as Donne observes, but also for his own life, following those suggestions in Meditation V.

Meditation VI is a classic description of the effect of the doctor's behavior on the emotions of his patient. It gives credence to the hypothesis that it is better to be open with a patient than to withhold information, even if it is adverse, while at the same time offering some justification for

---

70. Donne, *Devotions* (Sparrow), 17.
71. Donne, *Devotions* (Sparrow), 22.
72. Donne, *Devotions* (Sparrow), 22.
73. Donne, *Devotions* (Sparrow), 28.

a doctor's decision to conceal information from a patient: "I observe the *Phisician*, with the same diligence, as hee the *disease*; I see hee *feares*, and I feare with him: I overtake him, I overrun him in his feare, and I go the faster, because he makes his pace slow; I feare the more, because he disguises his fear, and I see it with the more sharpnesse, because hee would not have me see it. He knowes that his *feare* shall not disorder the practise, and exercise of his *Art*, but he knows that my *fear* may disorder the effect, and working of his practise."[74] It is a strong vignette, attesting to the anxiety of a patient when he is being examined, to the careful scrutiny to which a doctor's actions are given, and to the shrewdness of the patient who is able to pick up the feelings of the doctor, to recognize that he is dissembling, and to understand why the dissembling is used. His need to believe and trust in the ability of his doctor is reasserted at the end of the meditation. "As my *Phisicians* fear puts not him from his *practise*"[75]—he needs the physician to save him and he will not allow the possibility that emotional upset might hinder this savior. Here he chooses to see the physician as a diagnostic machine unaffected by emotions. It is therefore only natural that he experiences some emotional distress when this savior announces that he cannot do it alone, that he needs to consult with other doctors over the diagnosis.

This amount of distress that the doctor's need for consultation arouses in Donne is indicative of Donne's fear over the outcome of the disease; a fear which influences all his interactions with the doctor and which causes him to seemingly overreact. "There is *more feare*, therefore *more cause*. If the *Phisician* desire help, the burden grows great: There is a growth of the *Disease* then."[76] The other conclusion—that the doctor is inadequately trained for the case—is too threatening to be mentioned. And yet, it is obvious, from Donne's desire to show that the doctor is doing the right thing, that the other conclusion is being refuted. "Howsoever, his desiring of others, argues his *candor*, and his *ingenuitie*; if the danger be *great*, he *justifies* his proceedings, and he *disguises* nothing, that calls in *witnesses*; And if the danger bee not *great*, hee is not *ambitious*, that is so readie to divide the thankes, and the honour of that work, which he begun alone, with others."[77] This is followed by multiple examples of occasions when it is better to have more than one opinion—counsels of state, night watches, court cases—all profit from multiple aid. So why not counsels over disease? Again and again, he reassures himself "danger is not the more, and the providence is the more, wher

74. Donne, *Devotions* (Sparrow), 28.
75. Donne, *Devotions* (Sparrow), 29.
76. Donne, *Devotions* (Sparrow), 35.
77. Donne, *Devotions* (Sparrow), 35.

there are more *Phisicians*."⁷⁸ He continues to argue that "*Age* is a *sicknesse*, and *Youth* is an *ambush*; and we need so many *Phisicians*, as may make up a *Watch*, and spie every inconvenience."⁷⁹ His conclusion is that "therfore the more assistants, the better . . . as long as we can, let us admit as much *helpe* as wee can; Another, and another *Phisician*, is not another, and another *Indication*, and *Symptom* of death, but another, and another *Assistant*, and *Proctor* of *life*."⁸⁰ Here Donne states again his dual views of the doctor as helper and as symbol of illness—more doctors equal more illness. "Nor doe they so much feed the imagination with apprehension of *danger*, as the understanding with *comfort*; Let not one bring *Learning*, another *Diligence*, another *Religion*, but every one bring all, and, as many Ingredients enter into a Receit, so may many men make the Receit."⁸¹

At this point, there follows a vignette of other medical care delivered in the seventeenth century. This occurs in a digression by Donne in which he tells himself to be thankful that he has a doctor and consults, that he is not as those less fortunate who have no help: "How many are sicker (perchance) than I, and laid on their wofull straw at home (if that corner be a home) and have no more hope of helpe, though they die, then of preferment, though they live? Nor doe no more expect to see a *Phisician* then, then to bee an *Officer* after . . . for they doe but fill up the number of the dead in the Bill, but we shall never heare their *Names*, till wee reade them in the Booke of life, with our owne."⁸² These are the common people who have never risen in fame as Donne has, who are just numbers to him on the weekly bill of death. Later he will empathize with one who may fit this description, but now he sets himself above them. He continues his list of those less fortunate sick who cannot remain at home but must go to a hospital. "How many are sicker (perchance) than I, and thrown into *Hospitals*, where, (as a fish left upon the Sand, must stay the tide) they must stay the *Phisicians* houre of visiting, and then can bee but *visited*?"⁸³ This is Donne's image of a seventeenth-century hospital, which was often little better than a pest house and where people were more apt to become further infected and die than to get well. The image persisted until the nineteenth-century emphasis on sanitation changed the character of the institution. Finally, Donne describes the indigent who died on the streets of London, unable to even go to a hospital:

78. Donne, *Devotions* (Sparrow), 35.
79. Donne, *Devotions* (Sparrow), 35.
80. Donne, *Devotions* (Sparrow), 36.
81. Donne, *Devotions* (Sparrow), 36.
82. Donne, *Devotions* (Sparrow), 37.
83. Donne, *Devotions* (Sparrow), 37.

"How many are sicker (perchaunce) than all we, and have not this *Hospitall* to cover them, not this straw, to lie in, to die in, but have their *Grave-stone* under them, and breathe out the soules in the eares, and in the eies of passengers, harder than their bed, the flint of the street? That taste of no part of our *Phisick*, but a *sparing dyet*; to whom ordinary porridge would bee *Julip* enough, the refuse of our servants, *Bezar* enough, and the off-scouring of our Kitchen tables, *Cordiall* enough."[84] After this digression on the medical facilities available to the poor in the seventeenth-century England, Donne ends his meditation by thanking God that he can have helpers. The length at which he has analyzed these consults indicates the amount of anxiety that he is feeling.

In Meditation IX, he reacts to his examination by consulting doctors as he waits for them to diagnose and prescribe. "They have seene me, and heard mee, arraign'd mee in these fetters, and receiv'd the *evidence*."[85] Donne's image here is one of being on trial. This is followed by a medical school image. "I have cut up mine *Anatomy*, dissected my selfe, and they are gon to *read* upon me."[86] From these two images it is evident that Donne feels himself to be under examination such as a legal case or an anatomy lesson, not in a human sense. While he waits for the verdict, he thinks of the difficulty of diagnosing a disease, "how intricate a worke then have they, who are gone to *consult*, which of these *sicknesses* mine is, and then which of these *fevers*, and then what it would do, and then how it may be countermind."[87] It is the doctor as helper that is being referred to here. The very thought of the difficulty of diagnosis is too threatening to be further analyzed, and Donne drops it to go back to reassuring himself that the doctors are following the right course of action and that the course of action, to consult, indicates that things are not so critical; "But where there is room for *consultation*, things are not desperate. They *consult*; so there is nothing *rashly, inconsiderately* done; and then they *prescribe*, they *write*, so there is nothing *covertly, disguisedly, unavowedly* done."[88] He spends a great deal of time assuring himself that everything is all right, that the doctors are acting properly. He needs this reassurance, for he cannot act for himself and he is afraid of the outcome of the illness. It is very important for Donne to be able to believe this and he repeats his formula two more times, ending with "I am glad they know (I have hid nothing from them) glad they consult, (they hide nothing

---

84. Donne, *Devotions* (Sparrow), 37.
85. Donne, *Devotions* (Sparrow), 48.
86. Donne, *Devotions* (Sparrow), 48.
87. Donne, *Devotions* (Sparrow), 49.
88. Donne, *Devotions* (Sparrow), 49.

from one another) glad they write (they hide nothing from the world) glad that they write and prescribe *Phisick*, that there are *remedies* for the present case."[89] What a burden Donne is placing on the physicians here. He wants to be saved from his illness and he sees the doctors and their medicine in that role now.

All this while, Donne has been bolstering up his shaken confidence in the superhuman abilities of the doctor. He has now at least partially regained his confidence through the many arguments for having consultants and has placed his hope once again in the doctor as healer and the medicine as healing potent. And once again his faith is not sustained, for "they find the Disease to steale on insensibly, and endeavour to meet with it so."[90] The course of treatment and the selected medicine, chosen and prescribed after consultation with other physicians, has failed to halt the disease. At this point, the doctors decide to use cordials to keep the disease from attacking his heart, and to apply pigeons to draw vapors from his head. These attempts to stop the disease elicit pessimistic thoughts from Donne about the frailty of man and his vulnerability to destruction. There are no longer any positive statements about how he approves of the doctors' choice of medicine and treatment. He reacts with anger to their accusations that he brought the vapors on himself by his own melancholy. "Did I infuse, did I drinke in *Melancholly* into my selfe? It is my *thoughtfulnesse*; was I not made to *thinke*? It is my *study*; doth not my *Calling* call for that?"[91] Here he is angry with the authority, and a change in his relationship with his physicians is evident. They have not proved a superhuman defense against diseases. They have not effected a cure. And now they are threatening his identity as a thinker and writer by saying he is the cause of his complications. He may not dispute what they say, but he resents it. So, that when "the Sicknes declares the infection and malignity thereof by spots,"[92] he no longer has any faith in their ability to combat the disease: "This sicknesse declares itself by *Spots*, to be a malignant, and pestilentiall disease, if there be a *comfort* in the declaration, that therby the *Phisicians* see more cleerely what to doe, there may bee as much *discomfort* in this, That the malignitie may bee so great, as that all that they can doe, shall doe *nothing*; . . . It is a faint comfort to know the worst, when the worst is *remedilesse*; and a weaker than that, to know *much ill*, and not to know, that that is the worst."[93] Instead of responding to his diagnostic

---

89. Donne, *Devotions* (Sparrow), 50.
90. Donne, *Devotions* (Sparrow), 54.
91. Donne, *Devotions* (Sparrow), 69.
92. Donne, *Devotions* (Sparrow), 74.
93. Donne, *Devotions* (Sparrow), 74–75.

rash with optimism, asserting that the doctor can now combat the disease, he does not voice any hope in the doctor curing him, if the diagnosis is correct.

In giving up the image of his doctor as superhuman, he has not yet achieved a realistic view of his aid. The doctor is now seen as powerless against the disease, a mere commenter on the course of disease who has no powers to act. This view is reinforced by the doctors' announcement that Donne's illness has reached the critical days during which time the changes in a man's condition took place. He does not see the physicians helping him in this situation. Again, they are simply telling the stages of the illness. After this last reference to his doctors, Donne does not mention them again until after the episode with the bells, in which he reaches an acceptance of his sick state, and its attendant dependencies.

After he has become comfortable in his new situation, he seems to be able to accept his doctors in the more realistic role of helpers who have expertise in diagnosing and treating illness and gives up his grandiose hope of their superhuman powers and his morbid association of them with a symbol of his own impotence and illness. He observes that they cannot effect a cure if the propitious time has not occurred: "All this while the *Physitians* themselves have beene *patients*, patiently attending when they should see any *land* in this *Sea*, any *earth*, any *cloud*, any *indication* of *concoction* in these *waters*. Any *disorder* of mine, any *pretermission* of theirs, exalts the disease, accelerates the rages of it; no *diligence* accelerates the *concoction*, the *maturitie* of the *disease*; they must stay till the *season* of the sicknesse come, and till it be ripened of it selfe, and then they may put to their hand, to *gather* it before it *fall* off, but they cannot hasten the *ripening*."[94]

This is a much healthier view of the power of the physician. Donne's great fear has slackened and his need to see the physician as a savior has diminished. He has accepted the dependencies inherent in the sick state and no longer feels that his dependency on his doctor is a sign of impotency. He no longer feels impotent because he has recognized ways in which he can act in his sick state. He accepts the physicians' skill in following the disease and is glad to have their aid. "O how many farre more miserable, and farre more worthy to be lesse miserable than I, are besieged with this *sicknesse*, and lacke their *Sentinels*, their *Physitians* to *watch*, and lacke their *munition*, their *cordials* to *defend*."[95] He now sees their waiting during the critical days as a part of their plan to help, instead of as helplessness; and is optimistic over his ability, with them, to fight against his illness. "In me the *siege* is so

94. Donne, *Devotions* (Sparrow), 110–11.
95. Donne, *Devotions* (Sparrow), 112.

farre slackned, as that we may come to *fight*, and so die in the *field*, if I *die*, and not in a *prison*."⁹⁶

It is with this new attitude toward his doctors that he enters his convalescence. He never returns to his former need to view his physician as superhuman, or as a symbol of disease. He criticizes the doctors' choice of treatment—purging—without seeing this as a bad sign to be feared or as a prognostication of good news. The doctors, now fully human, are simply subject to being second-guessed by their patient, who acknowledges his former aid even while questioning the present treatment. "Without *counsell*, I had not got thus farre; without *action* and *practise*, I should goe no farther towards *health*. But what is the present necessary *action*? purging: A *withdrawing*, a violating of *Nature*, a *farther weakening*: O *deare price*, and O *strange* way of *addition*, to doe it by *substraction*."⁹⁷

Another indication of Donne's changed view of his doctors is the way he reacts to finally getting out of bed. Weakened by his illness—and perhaps by the purging as well—he has to be helped up and feels dizzy when he is on his feet. "I cannot *rise* out of my bed, till the *Physitian enable* mee, nay I cannot tel, that I am able to rise, till *hee tell* me so. I *doe* nothing, I *know* nothing of myself . . . Another tels mee, *I may rise*; and *I doe* so . . . I am readier to fall to the *Earth*, now I am up, than I was when I *lay* in the bed . . . I am *up*, and I seeme to *stand*, and I goe *round* . . . I seeme to *stand* to my *Company*, and yet am carried, in a giddy, and *circular motion*, as I *stand*."⁹⁸ This dependency on others causes him once again to go over his feelings of impotency, but the physician is no longer equated with that impotency. The feelings are there, but they are not generated by the presence of the doctors. Instead, they are attributed quite accurately to his weakened physical condition. He gives the doctors credit for their treatment and their help. "God prospers their practise, and he, by them, calls Lazarus out of his tombe, mee out of my bed."⁹⁹ Even when in Meditation XXII, Donne meditates on the lack of self-sufficiency of a human being, there is no anger directed toward the physician, or unrealistic hope given to him. "To cure the *sharpe accidents* of *diseases*, is a great worke; to cure the *disease it selfe* is a greater; but to cure the *body*, the *root*, the *occasion* of *diseases*, is a worke reserved for the great *Phisitian*, which he doth never any other way, but by *glorifying* these *bodies* in the next world."¹⁰⁰

96. Donne, *Devotions* (Sparrow), 112.
97. Donne, *Devotions* (Sparrow), 121.
98. Donne, *Devotions* (Sparrow), 127–28.
99. Donne, *Devotions* (Sparrow), 126.
100. Donne, *Devotions* (Sparrow), 136.

Finally, when he is told by the doctors of "the fearefull danger of relapsing," his feelings of fear do not include a projection of these fears to the doctor.[101] He describes his apprehension over having a relapse. He does not blame the doctor for this possibility and he does not see the doctor as being able to save him. Again, he is reacting to the doctor in his role as physician with realistic expectations.

Thus, in John Donne's *Devotions upon Emergent Occasions*, we may see at least four attitudes displayed toward the doctor. When Donne is in the throes of great anxiety over his illness, he sees the doctor a superhuman savior. At the same time, he sees him as a reminder of his disease and of his inability to cure that disease. This dual attitude persists until Donne himself reaches an acceptance of his changed condition. He first emphasizes his great fear by his extended need for his doctor to be all-knowing. (When there is a need to consult, it is evident from the degree of upset that Donne displays that he is reluctant to admit the possibility that the doctor may *not* be all knowing and may *not* effect a cure.) He needs his "Hercules against monsters" and each time this image is threatened by reality—i.e., the doctor is afraid, needs to consult, deliberates before prescribing, and prescribes medicine that does not cure—he works very hard to explain the event in a way that will not destroy his image of the physician. When his illness persists and he is no longer able to maintain this view, the reverse image surfaces—the doctor is then seen as no help at all—he is a person who diagnoses only to announce a name for the disease, or to announce that the disease has reached a critical stage—not to do anything about it. This second view is predominant during Donne's period of depression.

These two views of the physician as all powerful and powerless—views which parallel the stages of fear and depression—underline Donne's own feelings of impotency. He is in a situation where he cannot act to help himself, he must call in a physician and be dependent on this external aid for survival in a situation in which his very life is at stake. "We *have* the Phisician, but we *are not* the *Phisician*."[102] If the doctor is a reminder of Donne's impotency, he is also a reminder of the illness itself. "If the *Phisician* desire help, the burden grows great."[103] This view has a long traditional history. The bearer of bad news in ancient times was often equated with that news itself and either punished or killed. This incorporates the other traditional belief that to name a thing was to call it into being. Thus, a physician who is called to identify a disease is seen as the person who causes the disease itself and

---

101. Donne, *Devotions* (Sparrow), 139.
102. Donne, *Devotions* (Sparrow), 17.
103. Donne, *Devotions* (Sparrow), 35.

is therefore disliked. This view is the mirror image of the view that held that if one could give a threat a name, they could then control it. Hamlet, when seeking to address his father, exemplifies this belief:

> Thou comest in such a questionable shape
> That I will speak to thee: I'll call thee Hamlet,
> King, father, royal Dane: O, answer me!
> —*Hamlet.*, Act I, Scene IV, 43–45.[104]

Thus, the doctor, who is the messenger who brings bad news, who gives the threat a name, is also seen as the person who, knowing the name, can control the threat. Hence, the ambivalence towards the physician. To name the disease is to call it into being, and yet it is necessary to name it in order to control it.

Donne concentrates on the difficulty of naming the disease in Meditation IX: "If *ruine* were reduc'd to that one way, that Man could perish noway but by *sicknes*, yet his danger were infinit; and if *sicknes* were reduc'd to that one way, that there were no *sicknes* but a *fever*, yet the way were infinite still; it would overlode, and oppress any naturall, disorder and discompose any artificiall *Memory*, to deliver the *names* of severall *fevers*; how intricate a worke then have they, who are gone to *consult*, which of these *sicknesses* mine is, and then which of these *fevers*, and then what it would do, and then how it may be countermind."[105] Thus, Donne sees his doctor as part of the disease itself. The physician is the person responsible for identifying the disease and therefore giving it being. At the same time, the physician's identification offers the possibility of control. Donne's feelings of fear and impotency are projected onto the doctor, who is seen as a superman who can fight disease with weapons of medicine and conversely as impotent observer who understands the situation but is unable to rectify it.

These extreme views of the doctor's ability; combined with ambivalence toward his function, continue until after Donne reaches an acceptance of his sick role. He is then able to accept his dependency on the physician, to separate the disease itself from the diagnostician, and to relate to the physician with more realistic expectations. As long as he is working through his anxiety, however, he places unrealistic expectations on the doctor's ability to cure him, while simultaneously entertaining exaggerated fears over the doctor's ability to function competently. A totally "rational" view of the doctor does not appear during this period.

---

104. Shakespeare, *Hamlet*, Act 1, Scene IV, 43–45.
105. Donne, *Devotions* (Sparrow), 49.

A study of Donne's perception of his doctor during his illness offers insight for the physician today. If Donne's experience is generalizable, it follows that during the period of anxiety that follows the apprehension of bad news, the patient may need extensive support from those persons who are involved in their healthcare. The high potential for the physician to be seen as a savior at this time, however, should be recognized, and care be taken to not abuse this situation either by suggesting false hopes or by making decisions that could be made by the patient themselves. Furthermore, it should be recognized that while a patient is working through initial anxiety over the onset of illness, their anger, fear, depression, and hope over their own condition may be verbalized as opinions about the doctor's diagnosis and treatment of the disease. It is, therefore, normal and to be expected that the physician will experience these projections from their patient during this period. If they are prepared to recognize these feelings as expressions of anxiety, they will be able to respond to them as distress signals and thereby work directly on helping the patient's adjustment process rather than responding to them as personal attacks or demands. Just as Donne differentiated between crisis intervention and long–term cure, there may be at least two basic types of doctor–patient relationships: 1. the relationship that is possible while the patient is adjusting to a crisis, and 2. the relationship that is established for long–term illness management. In the first relationship, the physician may expect the patient to exhibit stress behavior that is perfectly normal for the crisis state. In the second relationship, a doctor may expect less exaggerated demands from their client and may, indeed, hope for less physician–directed decision making.

Finally, Donne's experience cries out to all healthcare personnel to remember the extreme vulnerability of the sick person and to respond to the manifestation of this vulnerability with empathy. If we remember that a sick person in a hospital is placed in a strange physical situation, deprived of normal food, dress, friends, and daily routine behavior, and tested and examined seemingly at will by personnel previously unknown to them, it becomes easy to understand that the need for security—far from being exaggerated—is entirely appropriate. The ministration to that need has long been recognized in the art of medicine.

Sick–Role Adaptive Behavior: Its Relationship to Donne's Emotional Evolution

Devotions upon Emergent Occasions presents a classic study of the emotions exhibited during an adaptation to the sick–role. John Donne experiences a sudden change in his health when he becomes ill from relapsing fever. He describes its physical effect graphically for us in the second Meditation: "In the same instant that I feele the first attempt of the disease, I feele the victory; In the twinckling of an eye, I can scarse see, instantly the tast is insipid, and fatuous; instantly the appetite is dull and desirelesse: instantly the knees are sinking and strengthlesse; and in an instant, sleepe, which is the *picture*, the *copie* of *death*, is taken away . . . I sweat againe, and againe, from the brow, to the sole of the foot, but I eat no bread, I tast no sustenance: Miserable distribution of *Mankind*, where one halfe lackes meat, and the other stomacke."[106] This illness causes immediate alterations to be made in his lifestyle. He is bedridden, isolated from his friends, and dependent upon a doctor. He loses his freedom of movement, his normal social behavior, and his independence in caring for himself.

In Meditation III, he reacts to this sudden alteration with strong disapproval. His bed is compared to a prison or a grave: "Scarse any prison so close, that affords not the prisoner two, or three steps."[107] "I . . . am in a close prison, in a sicke bed."[108] "A sicke bed, is a grave; and all that the patient saies there, is but a varying of his owne *Epitaph* . . . Miserable and . . . inhuman *posture*, where I must practise my lying in the *grave*, by lying still, and not practise my *Resurrection*, by rising any more."[109] This image of imprisonment is carried further to describe his weakened condition. "Strange fetters to the feete, strange Manacles to the hands, when the feete, and handes are bound so much the faster, by how much the coards are slacker; So much the lesse able to doe their Offices, by how much more the Sinewes and Ligaments are the looser."[110] He also objects to having to be dependent on the doctor, whom he calls a "Hercules against Monsters." "We *have* the <u>Phisician</u>, but we *are not* the *Phisician*. Heere we shrinke in our proportion, sink in our dignitie, in respect of verie meane creatures, who are *Phisicians* to themselves."[111]

---

106. Donne, *Devotions* (Sparrow), 6–7.
107. Donne, *Devotions* (Sparrow), 10.
108. Donne, *Devotions* (Sparrow), 16.
109. Donne, *Devotions* (Sparrow), 11.
110. Donne, *Devotions* (Sparrow), 11.
111. Donne, *Devotions* (Sparrow), 17.

Finally, in Meditation V, he objects to his separation from other people:

> As *Sicknes* is the greatest misery, so the greatest misery of sicknes, is *solitude*; when the infectiousnes of the disease deterrs them who should assist, from comming; even the *Phisician* dares scarse come. *Solitude* is a torment which is not threatened in *hell* it selfe . . . When I am dead, and my body might infect, they have a remedy, they may bury me; but when I am but sick, and might infect, they have no remedy, but their absence, and my solitude. It is an *excuse* to them that are *great*, and pretend, and yet are loth to come; it is an *inhibition* to those who would truly come, because they may be made instruments and pestiducts, to the infection of others, by their coming. And it is an *Outlawry*, an *Excommunication* upon the *Patient*, and seperats him from all offices not onely of *Civilitie*, but of *working Charitie*. A long sicknesse will weary friends at last, but a pestientiall sicknes averts them from the beginning . . . the height of an infectious disease of the body, is *solitude*, to be left alone: for this makes an infectious bed, equall, nay worse than a grave, that thogh in both I be equally alone, in my bed I *know* it, and *feele* it, and shall not in my *grave*.[112]

After his strong response to his changed lifestyle, Donne is faced with adapting to a sick-room routine. Instead of his normal daily activities, which included writing and delivering sermons, supervising the activities of St. Paul's Cathedral, caring for his children as his wife was dead by this time, and maintaining the social connections expected of the Dean of St. Paul's—activities which demanded the utilization of organizational skills and administrative expertise as well as theological knowledge and literary ability, all actively displayed—he must substitute waiting. Waiting for the doctors' arrival, watching the doctors for indications of the prognosis, noticing his physical condition, taking his medicine—activities which call for compliance and acceptance of other people's abilities rather than for the independence of action he had before. In his day-to-day survival, he previously had been accustomed to being self-reliant and independent. Now, in a life-threatening situation, his survival is dependent upon others. He must rely on their organization, intellectual ability, and scientific expertise. His world has narrowed to his bedroom, his social contact to that offered by his physicians; his ability to act channeled to following those physicians' directions.

---

112. Donne, *Devotions* (Sparrow), 22–24.

He must be patient, yet his skills are those of the initiator, and within the limits of this new situation, he uses as much of his old behavior as he can. He uses his skill as a writer to record how he feels during the illness. "To make my self believe that our life is something, I use in my thoughts to compare it to something, if it be like any thing that is something . . . This I do, by meditating, by expostulating, by praying; for since I am barred of my ordinarie diet, which is Reading, I make thee my exercises, which is another part of Physick."[113] He uses his analytical skill to help him accept scientifically the doctors' actions, and his theological expertise to give him spiritual perspective on his situation.

In concentrating in this way, on understanding the doctors' behavior, Donne is able for a while to define an area where he may achieve at least a temporary feeling of control, within a situation in which he is being acted upon. He follows the doctors' actions carefully—while analyzing each move until he is in agreement with it and thus can feel a part of the doctors' decision. If the doctor decides to consult, Donne discusses why this is a good thing to do rather than a threat. If he deliberates about the diagnosis, Donne analyzes the advantages to be gained from proceeding cautiously. In this way, Donne is able to maintain some feeling of participation in the management of his disease. The illusion lasts until the doctors' treatment fails to effect a cure. When this occurs, Donne gives up his involvement with the doctors' behavior and is overwhelmed with the depression that comes with an admission of his inability to help himself, compounded by his dwindling belief that the doctor can help him. He reaches the nadir in acceptance of his sick role when, having been told that his illness has reached the critical days, he lies awake in agitated depression, hearing the clock tell the hours.

At this point, an event outside of his sickroom causes Donne to begin a train of thought that ends in his acceptance of his situation. The passing bell, rung for a dying member of the parish, causes Donne to think that others may be in his situation, that he is sharing a situation with others, that it is a situation that all people experience, and that being interdependent is a part of being a human being. "No man is an *Iland*, intire of it selfe; every man is a peece of the *Continent*, a part of the *maine*."[114] After this signaling event, Donne appears to be comfortable in his role as a patient. He stops trying to be the doctor himself, and he accepts their aid. He hopes with their aid to recover, and he sees their medicines as helpful in his fight.

Thus, Donne experiences feelings of anger, fear, and depression in his adjustment to his sick role. It is interesting that these same feelings are

---

113. Coffin, *Complete Poetry*, 395–96.
114. Donne, *Devotions* (Sparrow), 98.

described by Donne during his convalescence when he is faced with re-assuming responsible, independent, self–reliant behavior. By this time, he has become comfortable in his role as a patient, and the physical change of getting out of bed, as well as the psychological change of being made responsible for his own health, causes him to feel impotent, also.

It has been demonstrated in Chapter 1 that the feelings that Donne experiences during his illness occur in response to change. In this chapter, the nature of the changes that the sick role demands have been pointed out. The physical change imposed by illness is seen to be only part of the multifaceted alteration of lifestyle imposed by the illness itself. The loss of Donne's occupational identity, his separation from that occupation and its structured routine, indeed his separation from the overall routine of normal daily life are a part of this alteration. The underlying loss of independence and control over his life is another part of this change. Donne must adapt to a sickroom routine, to a patient identity, and to a survival based on dependency upon others rather than independency. While this process of adjustment is going on, he displays anger, fear, and depression in response to this stress. When, however, he has grown accustomed to the routine, to his physical symptoms, and to the behavior expected of him as a patient, and has learned to function in that environment, he begins to feel less uncomfortable and accepts his sick role and its behavior, even while he continues to fight against the sickness itself. Thus, he is able to differentiate between the threat created by a new role and the threat of disease, and to see that accepting the situation that the disease creates is not to accept the disease itself.

Donne's Illness: The Demand for a Redefinition of Ultimacy

At the round earths imagin'd corners, blow
Your trumpets, Angells, and arise, arise
From death, you numberlesse infinities
Of soules, and to your scattred bodies goe,
All whom the flood did, and fire shall o'erthrow,
All whom warre, dearth, age, agues, tyrannies,
Despaire, law, chance, hath slaine, and you whose eyes,
Shall behold God, and never tast deaths woe.
But let them sleepe, Lord, and mee mourne a space,
For, if above all these, my sinnes abound,
'Tis late to aske abundance of thy grace,
When wee are there; here on this lowly ground,
Teach mee how to repent; for that's as good
As if thou'hadst seal'd my pardon, with thy blood.

HOLY SONNET VII, JOHN DONNE[115]

115. Grierson, *Metaphysical*, 86.

When John Donne is stricken with a sudden, critical illness, his first outcry is against the disruption of the order of his life. An event that he has neither anticipated nor even known of before has changed his habits and threatened his survival. He is, indeed, no longer in control of his life. "Variable, and therfore miserable condition of Man; this minute I was well, and am ill, this minute. I am surpriz'd with a sodaine change, and alteration to worse, and can impute it to no cause, nor call it by any name."[116] This loss of control comes in an area that Donne took pride in managing: his health. "We study *Health*, and we deliberate upon our *meats*, and *drink*, and *ayre*, and *exercises*, and we hew, and wee polish every stone, that goes to that building; and so our *Health* is a long and a regular work."[117] Despite good health practices and close maintenance of a proper diet, exercising, and keeping informed about the latest medical advances, he has become seriously ill. "But in a minute a Canon batters all, overthrowes all, demolishes all; a *Sicknes* unprevented for all our diligence, unsuspected for all our curiositie; nay, undeserved, if we consider only *disorder*, summons us, seizes us, possesses us, destroyes us in an instant."[118] The defenses that he had counted on have failed him and he is painfully aware of his inability to reconstruct these defenses, which, even if repaired, would no longer offer him the same sense of security.

Just as sudden illness makes him aware of his lack of ability to really order his life, it also makes him aware of his vulnerability to disease and to death. "O miserable condition of Man, which was not imprinted by *God*, who as hee is *immortall* himselfe, had put a *coale*, a *beame* of *Immortalitie* into us, which we might have blowen into a *flame*, but blew it out, by our first sinne . . . So that now, we doe not onely die, but die upon the Rack, die by the torment of sicknesse."[119] Furthermore, he recognizes that he is not only subject to disease itself, but to anxieties about the disease as well: "[We] are preafflicted, super–afflicted with these jelousies and suspitions, and ap-prehensions of *Sicknes* . . . O multiplied misery! we die, and cannot enjoy death, because wee die in this torment of sicknes; we are tormented with sicknes, and cannot stay till the torment come, but preapprehensions and presages, prophecy those torments, which induce that *death* before either come."[120]

Thus, in Meditation I, Donne is protesting against his inability to control his life. A disease about which he was ignorant, and therefore unable to

116. Donne, *Devotions* (Sparrow), 1.
117. Donne, *Devotions* (Sparrow), 1.
118. Donne, *Devotions* (Sparrow), 1.
119. Donne, *Devotions* (Sparrow), 1.
120. Donne, *Devotions* (Sparrow), 1.

anticipate and prevent, has threatened his existence. He is suddenly aware of his incomplete knowledge, of his vulnerability to disease and death, and of his susceptibility to anxieties over the approach of these threats. He can no more control his emotional response to disease, than he can control the disease itself. He is, therefore, from the very beginning of his book, stating his painful awareness of his human inadequacies that this illness has brought out. He is forced to admit that he is not like God—infinite, eternal, and unchangeable. He knows his problems are not problems peculiar to him; but, rather, characteristics of the human condition. All men experience sickness and death, feel anxiety over these events, and suffer from their incomplete knowledge in the decisions that they make. Thus, the distress that ends the first meditation is crying out against the entire human situation: "O perplex'd discomposition, O ridling distemper, O miserable condition of Man."[121]

Donne is presenting a universal situation illustrating the differences, the difficulties of the human condition through his own experience of that condition. The drama moves during the *Devotions* from the original viewpoint, in which Donne characterizes the frustrations of being a man and protests against his humanness, to the moment of the bells in which Donne accepts his humanity and exalts that interdependency experienced by all persons, who feel frustration when they seek to separate themselves from the integration achieved through shared experience, to substitute their own order for the larger order that this integration expresses.

The Donne who has cried out against not being God in his own life evolves, through suffering, which causes him to reevaluate his values, into an acceptance of his human characteristics. He is then free to do those human things through which men may experience the eternal now of God—being open to and sharing the feelings of other persons, helping them, and receiving help from them.

This acceptance is not to be equated with submission to an authority. It is achieved only after the positive apprehension of what it is to be a human being—both with its limitations and its unique qualities—and following this apprehension, an acceptance of this situation, with a desire to live within that orientation and to participate in the interactions of that community. Neither is this acceptance to be equated with a decision which Donne intellectually makes in order to restructure his life. Although, when examining the decision logically, it makes sense to order one's life in such a way that allows for the unexpected event, the possibility of sickness, the certainty of eventual death, and the emotional response to stress, Donne arrives at this awareness through physical experience, not an intellectual exercise.

---

121. Donne, *Devotions* (Sparrow), 2.

It is the physical experience which causes him to see that his orientation is inadequate, that his ultimate concern, as Tillich calls it, is off center, and that his value system must be restructured. Finally, Donne does not achieve acceptance by "getting control" of his life, or his emotions, or his illness. His attempts to do that, when successful, only temporarily relieve his situation and ultimately result in feelings of impotency when he inevitably fails. Instead, it is through losing control of his emotions, experiencing the distress caused by the loss of his old value system and the discomfort of his illness, and working through this distress, that Donne is purged of his need for his previous orientation and is able to be receptive to a new awareness of human relationships. Thus, his acceptance is not a submission, nor a philosophical reorganization, nor an act of "getting control" of himself. It comes after physical suffering, which disrupts the value system ordering his life and which results in strongly felt emotional distress. Donne does not will it, or devise it, or submit to it. It is insight achieved through suffering, both physical and emotional, and involves an apprehension of ultimate, universal order, an order which is indeed eternal and unchangeable and within which the human experience occurs. Union with this order is not achieved by attempts to establish lesser order systems, which end in frustration, but through participation in ultimacy, which comes when people relate to each other's needs empathetically.

Job and Donne: The Expansion of Awareness Through Suffering

He that dwelleth in the secret place of the most High shall abide under the shadow of the Almighty.

I will say of the Lord, He is my refuge and my fortress: my God; in him will I trust.

Surely he shall deliver thee from the snare of the fowler, and from the noisome pestilence.

He shall cover thee with his feathers, and under his wings shalt thou trust: his truth shall be thy shield and buckler.

Thou shalt not be afraid for the terror by night; nor for the arrow that flieth by day;

Nor for the pestilence that walketh in darkness; nor for the destruction that wasteth at noonday.

A thousand shall fall at thy side, and ten thousand at thy right hand; but it shall not come nigh thee.

Only with thine eyes shalt thou behold and see the reward of the wicked.

Because thou has made the Lord, which is my refuge, even the most High, thy habitation;

There shall no evil befall thee, neither shall any plague come nigh thy dwelling.

For he shall give his angels charge over thee, to keep thee in all thy ways.

They shall bear thee up in their hands, lest thou dash thy foot against a stone.

Thou shalt tread upon the lion and adder: the young lion and the dragon shalt thou trample under feet.

Because he hath set his love upon me, therefore will I deliver him: I will set him on high, because he hath known my name.

He shall call upon me, and I will answer him: I will be with him in trouble; I will deliver him, and honour him.

With long life will I satisfy him, and shew him my salvation.

—Psalm 91, *KJV*

A study of Donne's strong reaction to what he sees as underserved illness of which he is the innocent victim invites a comparison to the Job story. When Job, who has lived a good life and pleased God, suffers the misfortunes of losing his children and his material possessions and then is personally afflicted with disease, he, like Donne, cries out against the situation in which he finds himself. "Let the day perish wherein I was born, and the night in which it was said, 'There is a man child conceived' . . . For the thing which I greatly feared is come upon me, and that which I was afraid of is come unto me."[122] He would rather never have been born than be in this situation, in which he is covered with boils and unable to relieve his suffering. He is in acute misery and knows of no way to relieve it except to die which he is unable to do. This physical suffering, for which he is unprepared and with which he is unable to cope, is, however, the catalyst for the larger disturbance which Job suffers—the loss of the order by which he has organized his life.

The milieu in which Job has previously lived is described in the prologue to the book:

> There was a man in the land of Uz, whose name was Job; and that man was perfect and upright, and one that feared God, and eschewed evil. And there were born unto him seven sons and three daughters. His substance also was seven thousand sheep, and three thousand camels, and five hundred yoke of oxen, and five hundred she asses, and a very great household so that this man was the greatest of all the men of the east. And his sons went and feasted in their houses, every one his day; and sent and called for their three sisters to eat and to drink with them. And it was so, when the days of their feasting were gone about, that Job sent and sanctified them, and rose up early in the morning, and offered burnt offerings according to the number of them all: for Job said, It may be that my sons have sinned, and cursed God in their hearts. Thus did Job continually.[123]

This passage reveals a man in the prime of life who has lived a good life and been rewarded with a large family and material prosperity. He fears God, avoids evil, and is concerned for the spiritual welfare of his family. We are told later in the book that he has gained the respect of men older than himself, and that he has personally offered comfort to those who suffer adversity. It is this pattern of good deeds and prosperity that has been shattered by his illness. Although he has known intellectually that suffering comes to both good and bad, he has never experienced this in his own life

---

122. Job 3:3; Job 3:25.
123. Job 1:1–5.

and indeed his life has seemed to attest to the rewarding of virtue. Now, however, great misfortune culminating in physical misery has destroyed this orientation and with it, his sense of integration with the universe, with God. God, he cries has withdrawn himself. His apprehension of ultimacy is gone, and until he can know that ultimacy once again, he is at the mercy of the ungodly, subject to seeking to reorder his life while knowing that he cannot do this until he can once more experience the ultimacy which is God. In this situation of knowing that he has lost his relationship with God, that his apprehension of ultimate concern around which he ordered his life has been shattered by the problem of suffering, he is presented different ways of regaining order.

The first solution, offered by his wife, is the most simplistic. "Dost thou still retain thine integrity? Curse God and die."[124] This is the way of the nihilist who rejects any order, any concern for understanding events, who refuses to seek for order and lives a naturalistic existence. Job rejects this solution. "Thou speakest as one of the foolish women speaketh. What? Shall we receive good at the hand of God, and shall we not receive evil?"[125] He refuses to give up his belief in ultimate order and meaning. He verbalizes that good and evil events are both contained in the order that is God. "In all this did not Job sin with his lips."[126] While he continues to adhere intellectually to this belief, he has difficulty in integrating the fact of his own suffering into his life and the process of emotional integration is what occurs in the rest of the book.

A second solution to this anxiety caused by a loss of order, of orientation, is to accept the order that is offered by his friends and that he himself has previously adhered to, that is—to explain the presence of suffering as a punishment for wrong doing, to exclude suffering as a part of the human experience except as a correction of the ill deeds of man. "Remember, I pray thee, who ever perished, being innocent? Or where were the righteous cut off? Even as I have seen, they that plow iniquity, and sow wickedness, reap the same,"[127] observes Eliphaz the Temanite, who comes to visit him. Job rejects this reward and punishment explanation and refuses to categorize himself in that way. Wrong doing may result in suffering, but that is not the total explanation for suffering, for he has observed that the just suffer and the unjust go apparently unscathed. He recognizes that his friends offer a partial solution, one to which he can no longer adhere.

124. Job 2:9.
125. Job 2:10.
126. Job 2:10
127. Job 4:7–8.

A variation on the idea that suffering is punishment is the view of Job's fourth friend, Elihu, who sees suffering as sent as a means of educating a person and purifying him—that it is for his own good in the long run and will cause him to grow. This of course equates the stress with the growth. Men do grow out of stress, but the stress itself is not good. His partial answer of submission is also not accepted. The Lord calls it "words without knowledge," an attempt to bring order without the ability to see all the variables.[128]

A third solution is to accept the new order that includes suffering, both the suffering of the just as well as the unjust. Job, however, cannot do this through an act of will. He must first grieve for his old orientation before acceptance is possible. This grief process is accomplished in his answers to his friends. Job's personal reaction to the loss of meaning and order in his life is that of protest.

He expresses the wish to restore the old order, while he knows that this order cannot be restored. He is angry over his physical suffering which he feels to be undeserved. He is angry over the loss of the wholeness, of a sense of order that he had experienced that is now gone: "Why is light given to a man whose way is hid and whom God hath hedged in?"[129] He is also angry over his personal inability to restore this ordered world. This is the emotional response to his loss of order, and it follows the pattern of anger, fear, and depression that is seen in the Donne experience. Job does not want to give up his older order; he grieves for it as he slowly integrates his suffering into his value system and assimilates his new world view.

Job's first response to the loss of his physical health and with it the sense of order in his life, is anger. He curses his birth, the day when he first began to experience human existence: "Let the day perish wherein I was born, and the night in which it was said, There is a man child conceived. Let that day be darkness; let not God regard it from above, neither let the light shine upon it."[130] He remonstrates against physical suffering: "Wherefore is light given to him that is in misery, and life unto the bitter in soul; Which long for death, but it cometh not; and dig for it more than for hid treasures."[131] He cries out against man's inability to plan his own life and to control his own actions: "Why is light given to a man whose way is hid, and whom God hath hedged in? . . . For the thing which I greatly feared is come

---

128. Job 38:2.
129. Job 3:23.
130. Job 3:3–4.
131. Job 3:20–21.

upon me, and that which I was afraid of is come unto me. I was not in safety, neither had I rest, neither was I quiet; yet trouble came."[132]

The thing which Job fears is not only suffering, but a loss of his relationship with God, a loss of his orientation. It is this loss of relationship which he continues to grieve for throughout his emotional evolution. Just as Donne feels a loss of control over his emotions as well as his physical health, Job's loss of order has caused him to experience great anxiety: "For the arrows of the Almighty are within me, the poison whereof drinketh up my spirit: the terrors of God do set themselves in array against me."[133] He feels as if he has no hope for a return to good health: "What is my strength, that I should hope? and what is mine end, that I should prolong my life?"[134] "My days are swifter than a weaver's shuttle and are spent without hope."[135] His anxieties are even expressed in nightmares: "When I say, my bed shall comfort me, my couch shall ease my complaint; Then thou scarest me with dreams; and terrifiest me through visions: So that my soul chooseth strangling, and death rather than my life."[136] These feelings of impotency, expressed in anger, fear and despair, continue to recur in Job's later answers to his friends:

> Wherefore then hast thou brought me forth out of the womb? Oh that I had given up the ghost, and no eye had seen me! I should have been as though I had not been; I should have been carried from the womb to the grave. Are not my days few? Cease then, and let me alone, that I may take comfort a little. Before I go whence I shall not return, even to the land of darkness and the shadow of death; A land of darkness, as darkness itself, and of the shadow of death, without any order, and where the light is as darkness.[137]

Notice the imagery for death—"without any order." It is this confusion that Job is experiencing at this time. It is this death of relationship. To be without orientation is to be dead.

During this period of adjustment of his new situation, Job, like Donne, suffers from being cut off from his family and friends:

---

132. Job 3:23–26.
133. Job 6:4.
134. Job 6:11.
135. Job 7:6.
136. Job 7:13–15.
137. Job 10:18–22.

> He hath put my bretheren far from me, and mine acquaintance are verily estranged from me. My kinsfolk have failed, and my familiar friends have forgotten me. They that dwell in mine house, and my maids, count me for a stranger: I am an alien in their sight. I called my servant, and he gave me no answer; I intreated him with my mouth. My breath is strange to my wife, though I intreated for the children's sake of mine own body. Yea, young children despised me; I arose, and they spake against me. All my inward friends abhorred me: and they whom I loved are turned against me.[138]

And he, like Donne, sees the human relationship that is available to him in his four visitors, with the hope of a solution to his distress and with anger because their advice reminds him of his own predicament. When they fail him by not providing an answer that will bring order to his life once more, he directs his anger towards them in much the same way that Donne relates to his physician.

It is only after experiencing this grief process that a new apprehension of ultimacy is achieved by Job. In the two speeches of God, Job is shown the eternal order, that is not man centered, but of which man is a part. He sees in this new apprehension that it is not his place to impose explanations on ultimacy, that it is impossible for a finite man to explain this ultimacy. "Who is this that darkeneth counsel by words without knowledge?"[139] The order is there to be experienced, not explained; it is cosmic, universal, encompassing man's suffering, incorporating man himself in totality of expression. "I have heard of thee by hearing of the ear: but now mine eye seeth thee."[140] The distinction here is between intellectually accepted finite order and physical experience of eternal order. It is after Job has this experience of cosmic order that he is able to accept his new situation and to include it in his view of the universe.

After Job accepts the new order that includes suffering and the acceptance of his limitations as a human being, which he is able to apprehend after he has worked through his psychological response to the loss of his old orientation, he, too, is able to function in that new order as the human being that he is. The Job, who, when faced with a loss of ultimate orientation, turns inward, concentrating on his own condition and rejecting his own birth, is capable once more of concern for others. He prays for his friends, whose counsel has been clouded by the misapprehensions of a non–holistic view of life—a false ultimacy of rewards and punishments, of externally imposed

---

138. Job 19:13–19.
139. Job 38:2.
140. Job 42:5.

order rather that empathetic integration. This prayer of intercession is strangely parallel to Donne's prayer for the dying parishioner. Both prayers occur after the apprehension and acceptance of a new understanding of the order of ultimacy and man's relationship to and place in that ultimacy. Both prayers are an indication of the petitioners' reinvolvement with humanity, an expression of their human capability for positive action as opposed to their previous feelings of impotence. This action also parallels Job's behavior in the prologue, when he interceded for his sons. He is now able to continue in his old behavior within the new order, but with the difference that he has broadened his concern from his immediate family to his community of friends. In this sense Job's prayer may be seen as the intercession of a nabi, a religious leader, for those who are still seeking to apprehend ultimacy.[141]

The return to other centered relationships marks the beginning of Job's renewed relationship with a new understanding of ultimacy and order. It is physically demonstrated by a return to communication with his friends and by the return of his material prosperity, a prosperity which signifies externally that he is able to cope in his culture:

> And the Lord turned the captivity of Job when he prayed for his friends: also the Lord gave Job twice as much as he had before. Then came there unto him all his brethren, and all his sisters, and all they that had been of his acquaintance before, and did eat bread with him in his house: and they bemoaned him, and comforted him over all the evil that the Lord had brought upon him: every man also gave him a piece of money, and every man an earring of gold. So the Lord blessed the latter end of Job more than his beginning: for he had fourteen thousand sheep, and six thousand camels, and a thousand yoke of oxen, and a thousand she asses. He had also seven sons and three daughters.[142] . . . After this lived Job an hundred and forty years, and saw his sons, and his sons' sons, even four generations. So Job died, being old and full of days.[143]

The captivity may be read here as the impotency of action that occurs whenever one is primarily concerned for himself.

Thus, the Job story may be analyzed as a demonstration of what happens when an event occurs that shakes that idea of ultimate concern around which a person's life has been ordered. Job's world was arranged around a relationship with God, a view of the universe, that did not include extreme

---

141. Buber, *Prophetic Faith*, 196.
142. Job 42:10–13.
143. Job 42:16–17.

suffering by good people. When he, himself, loses his possessions, his family and his own health, his former view is destroyed. The order is gone. He can no longer apprehend it. God, he cries, has withdrawn himself. The problem then becomes how to achieve the order once more. The view presented by his wife—curse God and die—is immediately rejected. Job cannot imagine a world without order, without ultimacy. The view of his friends is also rejected. Their order is too narrow. It solves the problem of suffering by the reward and punishment theory, a theory that shuts out the fact that the just suffer and sinners are rewarded. It restores order by adhering to the old order, an explanation of ultimacy that Job recognizes as inadequate. Even the fourth friend, Elihu, who offers a less stern explanation—that suffering occurs for purposes of growth—is seen to be presenting an order that does not see life whole. Job knows intellectually that ultimacy is all inclusive and that suffering is indiscriminate, but he is not able to incorporate this knowledge into his own life experience. Until this time, he has lived a good life and prospered. The order of life was good. Now, in experiencing suffering himself, he emotionally rejects the new situation. He is angry over his condition, afraid of what will happen next, depressed over his inability to alter his state. He grieves for the old order as he had understood it. After he has passed through this grief process, in which he wishes things were as they were before and laments the apparent withdrawing of God, he apprehends the cosmic order of which he is a part. God shows him that ultimacy is not a state to be understood through intellectual explanation, but through emotional apprehension. With this fourth view of order—the order of ultimacy which is apprehended after Job has given up his old order, Job accepts his new situation, his new order, which includes suffering, not as punishment, or edification, but as a part of the whole experience of man. God is no longer withdrawn, Job is once more comfortable with the new structure and within this new structure he begins to function as a human being, who helps his friends as a part of that order.

Comparison of Job and Donne

Both Job and Donne move from men who seek to be like God—all knowing, all understanding, without illness—to men who see a new order in the universe, an order that includes suffering, men who accept the order and their place in it, and are able to act within this structure, to help other men. They move from men who are unable to act to men who are themselves intercessors, and this movement is achieved through a total emotional, physical and intellectual process rather than an intellectual act of will. Neither Donne nor Job are able to reestablish order. They both achieve an acceptance of the new order that is imposed on them *after* they become aware of a totality of experience that transcends their own situation. The "no man is an island" experience, in which Donne acknowledges the interdependency of all men and gives up his need to control his life, parallels Job's all-inclusive apprehension of ultimacy, of transcendent order. It is after this apprehension of eternal order that the present temporal order becomes incorporated in their world, and their intellectual and emotional disturbance resolves into the peace of God in which their will is one with the will of God. This is accomplished not by an act of will to achieve or to submit or to control, but through ultimate reality, emotionally apprehended, following a period of grieving for a temporal order that has been shattered.

The experience of Job and Donne may thus be shown to follow a basic pattern of adjustment to a new order that has been imposed on them. The ways in which they express their discomfort and cope with their distress reflect the different cultural backgrounds within which these experiences occur, and the specific adaptation of each man to his overt culture.

The external plots of the two works display many parallels. Job is a successful man who suddenly experiences misfortune and illness. He is physically ill, his environment has changed from a prosperous household to an ash heap, he is cut off from his old social and familial interchange. This abrupt change shatters his old view of the world, in which he has seen prosperity as a reward and suffering as a punishment from God, a view that has been supported by his socio-economic group within the general culture.[144] While in this state of confusion, his communication with human beings is limited to his wife and four friends, who seek to help him cope with his situation. In an effort to reorganize his world, he rejects the old view presented by his friends, that suffering is the result of sin, a view which is incompatible with his personal experience. At the same time, he laments the loss of relevancy which he had felt while secure in this old system. After Job experiences feelings of anger, loneliness, fear, and depression, God appears in a whirlwind—the cosmic order is apprehended where chaos had been—and he is able to see himself in relationship to the order outside the localized comprehension of man. From this apprehension of a greater order, Job is able to accept his new framework. He stops concentrating on his personal situation and prays for the welfare of his friends, who are still seeking to explain their relationship to God from the old constricted viewpoint of reward and punishment which is their world. After this intercession, Job returns to human society which succors him by helping him financially and

---

144. Gordis, *God and Man*.

supports him by empathizing with his misery. In this milieu, he prospers for many years, dying at last of old age.

Donne is also a successful man. A theologian, he has achieved, by his own abilities, recognition in his profession by being made Dean of Saint Paul's Cathedral. His sudden and severe illness, which changes his health, his daily life patterns, his physical surroundings, and his social interaction, also shatters the illusion of independent control over his life that he has adhered to and that he has ordered his life around. Except for his physicians' visits, he, too is largely shut off from human contact during this period of readjustment. After experiencing anger, loneliness, fear, and depression over his new situation and the lack of control and independence that it represents, Donne apprehends a new order of human interdependency, through his spiritual interaction with the dying parishioner. After this awareness of the community of human suffering, he is able to accept his own dependent situation as a part of that larger order. He then stops concentrating on himself, and participates in this community by praying for the dying man. This act marks the beginning of Donne's functioning within the new order. He subsequently regains his health and is restored to his former state of independence. Like Job, his old life patterns continue, it is his orientation, his apprehension of ultimacy that has been enlarged during the experience.

Tradition of the Individual is Reflected in his Experience

Within these two similar plots, the experience of each man and the final awareness is appropriate to his historical, cultural, and religious milieu. For example, the written Job story has been attributed to dates as late as 500 to 300 B.C., a time in which men were working on understanding their personal relationship to God.[145] It is, therefore, in these terms—a loss of relationship, that Job speaks of the confusion he feels by a sudden change in situation, and his apprehension of cosmic order is in terms of his renewed relationship with God. Donne's experience, however, occurs 2,000 years later, after 1,700 years of Christianity, and his confusion and resolution are expressed in terms that are appropriate to that culture. His understanding of ultimacy is in terms of the Christian experience, in which God is known through interrelationships of men who participate in eternity through the interdependency of actor and sufferer. Each man's heightened understanding is thus within his tradition, although the general pattern is the same.

---

145. Gordis, *God and Man*.

View of God and Suffering

Both Donne and Job, working within their milieu, reject the traditional view of God and of suffering that they held prior to their sudden illness. Job, the greatest of all the men of the East, has been taught to see God's hand and God's purpose in temporal events. However, in ascribing suffering to a reward and punishment explanation, the anthropomorphic God who is described in terms of human personality in order to be comprehended by human beings has come to be seen as literal myth.[146] The symbolism has been lost and ultimate concern has been confined to a judge, limited to human interpretation of order. It is with this literal application, that has narrowed from the general concept of divine order that Job must deal, and it is only after much suffering and emotional distress that he finally establishes the difference between a meaningful relationship with ultimacy and a legalistic reading of each event in terms of ultimate approval and disapproval.

The traditional view of suffering as the punishment for some misdeed is also rejected by Job. Once again, the desire to attribute all things to God has been literally applied and results in faulty conclusions, and again, it is after physically experiencing a situation that negates those conclusions and struggling with the diffuse anxiety that accompanies this negation, that Job apprehends an order that includes suffering without negating God or man.

Donne, who must work from a background steeped in Christian tradition, also rejects the literal application of that tradition. He also is faced with tenets of reward and punishment, now carried into the next world. Christ's suffering had been defined as sacrificial and an act by which eternal life was achieved through literal resurrection in another world. Martyrs had followed this route, the sick had been sustained by it, enduring pain and hoping for surcease after death. Suffering had become a means to a literal end, while its meaning on this earth was defined in the same scheme of reward and punishment against which Job fought. Donne, however, who suffers terribly, cannot explain his illness in these cause–and–effect relationships. He protests literally over his misery. Finally, he is less than positive over his eternal salvation, despite his protestations of belief. Yet, Donne moves from this literal tradition to the point in which he apprehends the universality and the interdependence of all men who act and suffer; and by participating empathetically in his human experience, he partakes of the eternal now. The passion of Christ, in which the sharing of human suffering is the way to overcome the limitations of time, has been personally experienced by Donne. The tradition has been given new meaning, and suffering, rather than being

---

146. Tillich, *Dynamics of Faith*, 50–54.

a thing to be endured until death offers relief, or an experience to be denied if at all possible, has been reaffirmed as a central part of the human experience through which men participate in eternal moments of community.

In like manner, Donne works away from a traditional Christian concept of God as literal Creator, Savior, and Holy Spirit. In this view, Christ came to save men from their sins in this world, God the Father will judge men fit or unfit for eternal life in the next world, and the Holy Spirit is sent to help men achieve this otherworldly salvation. This view was further narrowed through interpretations to equate freedom from sin with inner control, which could be achieved by the help of the Holy Spirit. The ultimate end of this behavior was removal from this world to heaven. Yet the experience of ultimacy that Donne has occurs when he gives up trying to control, realizes his interdependency on other persons, and physically participates in that interaction. Salvation is not attained through submission or control, but through acceptance of others; it is not a reward for a good life, but a series of empathetic relationships in which that ultimacy that is God is known through human interaction. Thus, Donne's desire for temporal order in his life ends in his participation in eternal order, in experiencing the eternal now of suffering and succoring; and Job's cry for a renewed relationship with God is answered by an apprehension of cosmic order and concludes in his reestablishing his relationship with his friends. The apprehension of a new ultimacy permits the acceptance of a new situation, with its new order, in which, in both cases, the man's ability to function holistically in it is indicated by his demonstrated capacity for expression of human concern for others.

Donne's Relationship to God

Donne's original cry of anguish refers to the recognized loss of ability to order his life. He does not, as Job, lament his inability to relate to God during this time of stress. Rather, the very form of his writing, a series of devotions, in which two of the three major parts—the expostulation and the prayer—are directed to God, would seem to reinforce the fact that this relationship is of major solace to him during his distress. Certainly, he makes a point of stating his belief in God directly after he has expressed fear and depression in his meditations. An examination of the three major parts, however, has been shown to yield a progression of internal integration of thought: whereas in the pre–bell devotions, the meditations are distinct from the expostulation and prayer, during Donne's apprehension of shared suffering and his subsequent acceptance, the thought of the meditation is integrated with the other sections into a holistic expression of human interaction and empathy.

This fusion of his physical and religious thought may point, then, to a change in his physical and psychological adaptation. In fact, if this hypothesis is examined from the point of view of Donne's milieu, his early relationship to God as expressed in the Devotions I–XV, and his apprehension of God as he listens to the passing bell, it becomes apparent that he indeed grows in spiritual awareness during this time from a person who compartmentalized his life so that God and man interact only on theological terms, to a person who physically experiences God in his relationship with the dying parishioner.

Fragmentation of religious and physical experience by Donne seems at first to be a contradiction in terms, for his poetry is noted for its use of religious imagery in the description of physical union and conversely, in its use of physical terms to describe religious experience:

> And by these hymnes, all shall approve
> *Us Canoniz'd* for Love:
> And thus invoke us; You whom reverend love
>   Made one anothers hermitage;
> You, to whom love was peace, that now is rage;
>   Who did the whole worlds soule contract, and drove
>   Into the glasses of your eyes
>   (So made such mirrors, and such spies,
> That they did all to you epitomize,)
>   Countries, Townes, Courts: Beg from above
>   A patterne of your love!
>   —The Canonization, John Donne[147]

> Batter my heart, three person'd God; for you
> As yet but knocke, breathe, shine, and seeke to mend;
> That I may rise, and stand, o'erthrow mee,'and bend
> Your force, to breake, blowe, burn, and make me new.
> I, like an usurpt towne, to'another due,
> Labour to'admit you, but Oh, to no end,
> Reason your viceroy in mee, mee should defend,
> But is captiv'd and proves weake or untrue.
> Yet dearely'I love you,'and would be loved faine,
> But am betroth'd unto your enemie:
> Divorce mee,'untie, or breake that knot againe,
> Take mee to you, imprison mee, for I
> Except you'enthrall mee, never shall be free,
> Nor ever chast, except you ravish mee.
>   —Holy Sonnet XIV, John Donne[148]

---

147. Coffin, *Complete Poetry*, 13.
148. Grierson, *Metaphysical*, 88.

These poems are representative of his style, which juxtaposes very different images in the recreation of an experience. It is a juxtaposition that retains the tension evoked by the shock of dissimilar elements that he uses to express an experience; a technique that invites intellectual resolution but remains emotionally taut. The apprehension that the images *do* partake of the same experience in different situations suggests the use of this technique, while the fact that they are seen by the poet as different and conflicting prevents that integration. Thus, we experience stimulation but not fusion. The words, then, reflect the intellectual experience of the poet while simultaneously attesting to his inability to integrate his diverse areas of expertise.

The same phenomena is to be observed in the *Devotions upon Emergent Occasions*. Donne writes from a background of intellectual achievement in secular and religious studies. He juxtaposes these areas in his treatment of his illness. In the Meditations, he analyzes his situation from a scientific and secular orientation. In the Expostulations and Prayers, he re-expresses his situation, using religious terms and theological expertise. Both methods reveal Donne's psychological stages of response to illness. However, despite the extension of Donne's distress to the spiritual realm, the two latter sections remain distinct in their presentations. The unity, as in the poetry, is largely intellectual and imposed by external structure.

What does this indicate about Donne's understanding of religion? Of his relationship to God? We know that religion was a major influence in the life of Donne. During his childhood and adolescence, it was his Roman Catholicism that separated him from participation in the general culture of the English Renaissance, and it was Roman Catholicism that kept him from being permitted to receive a degree from the universities. Separate from the English church, it separated those who adhered to it. Thus, from his earliest memory, religion had been an important part of his life, and yet it had been apart from his secular experience. The external pattern imposed by persecution was incorporated into his later treatment of religion, both in his writing and in his life, and his years as an Anglican continued this pattern. Thus, it is not unusual for Donne to fragment his emotions in the *Devotions upon Emergent Occasions* into sections which first analyze the physical discomfort and emotional turmoil experienced during his illness and then explicate the spiritual implications of those needs.

This explanation of the natural fragmentation of Donne's experience may be followed still further in an attempt to understand Donne's concept of God during his illness. Donne's position as a theologian and as the Dean of Saint Paul's Cathedral limits his ability to announce overtly, as Job does, that he feels the withdrawing of God. Christian theology clearly states that God is ever-present and that man only experiences separation from Him by some act of sin for which man is responsible. If we use these terms in the sense of Tillich's literal myth, instead of in the broader symbolic significance in which they were formed, we can see Donne's problem. To admit a loss of relationship is to admit a failing by Donne to maintain that relationship. So, Donne continues to expostulate and pray, to avow his trust in God, while he emotionally and physically exhibits an inability to trust anyone, and strongly resists his dependent situation. He does not admit his non–relationship because he cannot accept the guilt implied by the literal system. He also cannot speak of this because he needs God to save him in his distress just as he needs the physician to cure him. If he says that he feels estranged from God, how, literally, can an estranged God rescue him; furthermore, this all-powerful God is in the position of deciding on Donne's eternal fate. Donne certainly would not wish to appear to indicate that he is less than confident in his relationship and in his salvation. Finally, he cannot verbalize his loss of relationship because the order that he has previously experienced has been a fragmented order, in which religion and God have remained separated from his physical experience and have, indeed, often represented opposite viewpoints. Thus, he has never had the integrated religious experience that was Job's, and his belief in eternal reward and punishment makes him unable to verbalize his distress directly.

Chaucer's Retractions

Wherefore I biseke yow mekely, for the mercy of God,

that ye preye for me that Crist have mercy on me and foryeve me my giltes;

and namely of my translacions and enditynges of worldly vanitees,

the whiche I revolke in my retracciouns: . . .

the tales of Caunterbury, thilke that sownen into synne; . . .

and many another book, if they were in my remembrance,

and many a song and many a lecceherous lay;

that Crist for his grete mercy foryeve me the synne . . .

so that I may been oon of hem at the day of doom that shulle be saved.

Qui cum patre, et Spiritu Sancto vivit et regnat Deus per omnia secula. Amen.

Heere is ended the book of the tales of Caunterbury, compiled by
Geffrey Chaucer, of whos soule Jhesu Crist have mercy. Amen
—*THE CANTERBURY TALES*, GEOFFREY CHAUCER 1393–1400[149]

149. Chaucer, *Works*, 265.

God–Donne Relationship: Crisis Needs—Formula or Process

I

Wilt thou forgive that sinne where I begunne,
    Which is my sin, though it were done before?
Wilt thou forgive those sinnes, through which I runne,
    And do run still: though still I do deplore?
        When thou hast done, thou hast not done,
            For, I have more.

II

Wilt thou forgive that sinne which I'have wonne
    Others to sinne? and, made my sinne their doore?
Wilt thou forgive that sinne which I did shunne
    A yeare, or two: but wallowed in, a score?
        When thou hast done, thou hast not done,
            For I have more.

III

I have a sinne of feare, that when I have spunne
    My last thred, I shall perish on the shore;
Sweare by thy selfe, that at my death thy sonne
    Shall shine as he shines now, and heretofore;
        And, having done that, Thou haste done,
            I feare no more.

    — A Hymn to God the Father, John Donne, 1623–24[150]

---

150. Grierson, *Metaphysical*, 93.

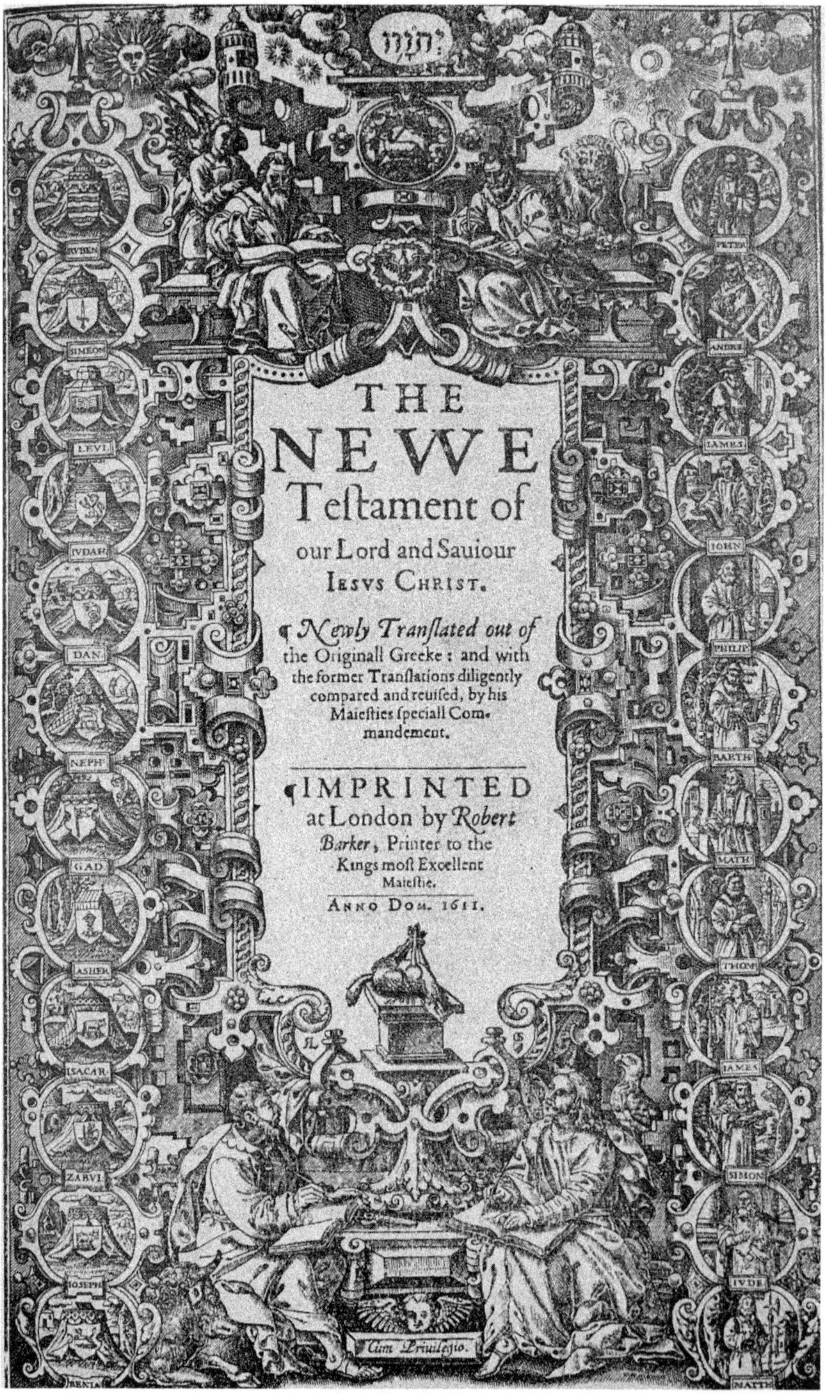
THE
NEWE
Testament of
our Lord and Sauiour
Iesvs Christ.

¶ *Newly Translated out of* the Originall Greeke: and with the former Translations diligently compared and reuised, by his Maiesties speciall Commandement.

¶ IMPRINTED at London by *Robert Barker*, Printer to the Kings most Excellent Maiestie.

Anno Dom. 1611.

Cum Priuilegio.

A study of the Expostulation and Prayers of John Donne's *Devotions upon Emergent Occasions* reveals changes in Donne's view of God that parallel the various psychological stages that Donne experiences during his illness. When Donne is in the throes of adjusting to his new situation, when his old order has been destroyed, and when he is responding to feelings of impotency with anger, fear, and depression, he sees God as capable of saving him from his distress. At the same time, he sees God as the person who is responsible for his illness, which is seen to be sent as an indication of God's anger, as a method of correction, as a means of purgation, and as a way of purification. The simultaneous views of God as savior from and instigator of illness correspond to the views that Donne exhibits during the same period of time toward his physician; who, it may be recalled, is seen as a powerful person and as a reminder of dependency. A third view of God as a friend who is present during his separation from others is also expressed about the physician. When, however, Donne accepts his situation, after becoming aware of the larger order of suffering, he no longer speaks of God in these all-powerful terms. Instead, it as a God of order who now is addressed. Thus, it seems that Donne's awareness of God is influenced by his emotional condition, and that just as in his relationship with the doctor, while he is in a state of emotional and physical distress following the loss of a value system, he sees his situation from an intensely personal viewpoint that projects his hopes and fears onto God so that God is seen to exhibit those qualities which Donne most needs or fears. When, however, Donne has accepted his situation and is capable of coping within his new environment, his image of God becomes much less charged with fear and expectancy and reveals a sense of relationship to cosmic order that is not seen prior to acceptance.

God as the Instigator of and Savior from Sickness

Donne's view of God as the instigator of the sickness for a particular purpose is first seen in Expostulation II, where he expresses fear that God is showing his anger through sickness:

> *My God, my God*, why comes thine anger so fast upon me? Why dost thou melt me, scatter me, poure me like water upon the ground so instantly? Thou staidst for the first world, in *Noahs* time, 120 yeres; thou staidst for a rebellious generation in the wildernes, 40 yeres, wilt thou stay no minute for me? Wilt thou make thy *Processe*, and thy *Decree*, thy *Citation*, and thy *Judgement* but one act? Thy *Summons*, thy *Battell*, thy *Victorie*, thy *Triumph*, all but one act; and lead me captive, nay, deliver me

> captive to death, as soon as thou declarest me to be *enemy*, and so cut me of even with the drawing of thy sword out of the scabberd, and for that question, *How long was he sicke?* leave no other answere, but that the hand of death pressed upon him from the first minute? . . . shall thy breath in this Chamber breathe *dissolution*, and *destruction, divorce*, and *separation*?[151]

Donne, however, cannot tolerate this view that God is angry with him, with its accompanying concept of separation from God, and in the prayer that follows the expostulation, he modifies this view to the more tolerable one of correction. "Interpret thine owne worke, and call this sicknes, correction, and not anger, and there is soundnes in my flesh."[152] In the third prayer, he again asserts his view of sickness as a correction and further develops this idea to seeing suffering as a purification for past sin, a purgation of past promiscuity:

> Forget my bed, *O Lord*, as it hath beene a bedde of sloth, and worse then sloth, Take mee not, *O Lord*, at this advantage, to terrifie my soule, with saying, Now I have met thee there, where thou hast so often departed from me; but having burnt up that bed, by these vehement heates, and washed that bed in these abundant sweats, make my bed againe, *O Lord*, and enable me according to thy command, *to commune with mine owne heart upon my bed, and be still*. To provide a bed for all my former sinnes, whilest I lie upon this bed . . . and when I have deposed them in the wounds of thy Sonn, to rest in that assurance, that my Conscience is discharged from further *anxietie*, and my soule from further *danger*, and my Memory from further *calumny*.[153]

Thus, Donne offers a description of the way he feels about himself at the onset of his illness. His conscience is filled with anxiety, he feels that his soul is in danger and is wracked with guilt when he remembers former sins. This is not Job, who had known the security and prosperity of a life lived within a value system that was integrated with his behavior and which no longer worked. Rather, it is the cry of a man whose life experience has been fragmented, whose actions do not always reflect his religious beliefs, who recognizes this incongruity, suffers guilt feelings because of this inconsistency, and yet never resolves the conflict between his behavior and his avowed belief. It is a terrible state to be in, in which he is desperate, needs and desires the peace of God which he has never known, clings to any form

---

151. Donne, *Devotions* (Sparrow), 7–8.
152. Donne, *Devotions* (Sparrow), 9.
153. Donne, *Devotions* (Sparrow), 15.

of possible relationship to God that he can imagine, and experiences mental anguish over the demands placed on him by his various images of God.

In these early expostulations and prayers, the might of God and his superhuman abilities are also emphasized. It is significant that Donne chooses this quality in a time in which he is experiencing great anxiety over his situation. God is addressed in Prayers III, IV, and VI as "Most mightie, and most merciful."[154] God is recognized as the cause of the illness in Expostulation II and III, and in Prayer IV, he is seen to have abilities both to protect Donne from the physician—"Keepe me back, *O Lord*, from them who mis–professe artes of healing the *Soule*, or of the *Body*, by meanes not imprinted by thee in the *Church*, for the *soule*, or not in *nature* for the *body*."[155]—and to help the physician heal—"for my temporall health, prosper thine *Ordinance*, in their hands who shall assist in this sicknes, in that manner, and in that measure, as may most glorifie thee."[156] In addition to being able to protect Donne from doctors and to help the work of good doctors, God is also called upon to personally heal Donne himself. "*Thy Sonn went about healing all manner of sicknesses* . . . *Vertue went out of him, and he healed all*, all the multitude . . . he left no relikes of the disease; and will this universall *Phisician* passe by this *Hospitall*, and not visit mee? not heale me? not heale me wholy?"[157] God the Savior is also referred to in Prayer V: "So whether it bee thy will to continue mee long thus, or to dismisse me by death, be pleased to afford me the helpes fit for both conditions, either for my weak stay here, or my finall transmigration from hence . . . *Be* my salvation, and *plead* my salvation; *work* it, and *declare* it; and as thy *Triumphant* shall be, so let the *Militant Church* bee assured, that thou wast my *God*, and I thy servant, *to*, and *in* my consummation."[158]

This appeal to God to directly help him is followed by another plea for God to help the doctor heal him. "Blesse thou the learning, and the labours of this Man, whom thou sendest to assist me; and since thou takest mee by the hand, and puttest me into his hands . . . prosper him, and relieve me, in thy way, in thy time, and in thy measure. *Amen*."[159]

Expostulation VI continues the view of an all-powerful God, but with emphasis once again on the God who has the power to discipline through sickness, rather than on his power to save from sickness. Donne is afraid

---

154. Donne, *Devotions* (Sparrow), 20.
155. Donne, *Devotions* (Sparrow), 20–21.
156. Donne, *Devotions* (Sparrow), 22.
157. Donne, *Devotions* (Sparrow), 21.
158. Donne, *Devotions* (Sparrow), 27.
159. Donne, *Devotions* (Sparrow), 27.

that his illness is sent by God as a correction for his past behavior. "I am abundantly rich in this, that I lye heere possest with that feare, which is *thy feare*, both that this sicknesse is thy immediate correction, and not meerely a *naturall accident*; and therefore fearefull, because *it is a fearefull thing to fall into thy hands*."[160] And again he moves to modify correction into purgation. "And when thou shalt have inflamd, and thawd my former coldnesses, and indevotions, with these heats, and quenched my former heates, with these sweats, and inundations, and rectified my former presumptions, and negligences with these fears, bee pleased, *O Lord*, as one, made so by thee, to thinke me fit for thee."[161]

With the idea of correction comes the idea of submission to the correction. "Let mee not therefore, *O my God*, bee ashamed of these *feares*, but let me feele them to determine, where his feare did, in a present submitting of all to thy will."[162] Donne continues to state that he wishes to submit his will to that of God, but he is neither emotionally nor mentally able to do this and his avowed desire to submit becomes an exercise in what he believes he *ought* to do *if* the sickness is a *correction*. His actual acceptance, later in the *Devotions*, is on a holistic basis and only after that does his avowed desire to submit actualize itself not as submission but as acceptance.

As the Expostulations move into Donne's period of fear, which is handled by coping mechanisms, and depression, which is unrelieved by these methods, he continues to refer to his illness as a form of correction by God, while he rarely refers to God's ability to save him. As the hope of being saved diminishes, the avowed desire to submit to the correction grows. His reiteration of this desire is indicative of his unstable state. The view of illness as disciplinary, to which the correct response is submission, appears in Prayer VII: "I humbly beseech thee, to make this correction, which I acknowledg to be part of my *daily bread*, to tast so to me, not as I would, but as thou wouldest have it taste, and to conform my tast, and make it agreeable to thy will. Thou wouldst have thy corrections tast of *humiliation*, but thou wouldest have them tast of *consolation* too; taste of *danger*, but tast of *assurance* too."[163] The prayer ends with more references to correction. At this time, however, in which the doctor is seeking consults, Donne still hopes that his illness can mean Mercy rather than correction:

> Let me think no degree of this thy correction, *casuall*, or without *signification*; but yet when I have read it in that language, as it

---

160. Donne, *Devotions* (Sparrow), 33.
161. Donne, *Devotions* (Sparrow), 34.
162. Donne, *Devotions* (Sparrow), 34.
163. Donne, *Devotions* (Sparrow), 40.

is a *correction*, let me translate it into another, and read it as a *mercy*; and which of these is the *Originall*, and which is the *Translation*; whether thy *Mercy*, or thy *Correction*, were thy primary and original intention in this sicknes, I cannot conclude, though death conclude me; for as it must necessarily appeare to bee a *correction*, so I can have no greater argument of thy *mercy*, then to die in *thee*, and by that death, to bee united to him, who died for me.[164]

By Prayer IX, however, Donne is calling his sickness a form of painful treatment for the soul, which has been prescribed by God the Physician. "Take me then, *O blessed*, and *glorious Trinitie*, into a *Reconsultation*, and prescribe me any *phisick*; If it bee a long, and painful holding of this *soule* in *sicknes*, it is *phisick*, if I may discern thy hand to give it, and it is *phisick*, if it be a speedy departing of this *Soule*, if I may discerne thy hand to receive it."[165] And by Prayer XI, which ends the devotion on the frailty of the heart that initiates Donne's period of depression, Donne has given up hope of being physically saved by God and is working once more on trying to submit to God's will:

> When thy blessed *Sonne* cryed out to thee, *My God, my God, why hast thou forsaken mee?* thou diddest reach out thy hand to him; but not to deliver his *sad soule*, but to receive his *holy soule*: Neither did hee longer desire to hold it of thee, but to recommend it to thee. I see thine hand upon me now, O Lord, and I ask not why it comes, what it intends; whether thou wilt bidde it stay still in this *Body* for some time, or bidd it meet thee this day in *Paradise*, I aske not, not in a *wish*, not in a *thought*: *Infirmitie of Nature, Curiositie of Minde*, are tentations that offer; but a silent, and absolute obedience, to thy will, even before I know it, is my *Cordiall*.[166]

Here again, Donne shows where he is emotionally, by his enumeration of things that impede submission:

1. infirmity of nature—i.e., his physical condition from which he still wishes to be cured; and
2. curiosity of mind—i.e., his desire to intellectually understand what is happening to him.

---

164. Donne, *Devotions* (Sparrow), 41.
165. Donne, *Devotions* (Sparrow), 54.
166. Donne, *Devotions* (Sparrow), 67.

He is not ready physically or intellectually to accept his situation, while his theology tells him that he should do this, and he is trying to achieve submission, despite his adverse feelings.

The Twelfth Prayer, in correspondence with the meditation that precedes it, introduces the element of hope briefly again, as Donne asks God the Savior to help the doctor's treatment to heal him. "Prosper I humbly beseech thee, this means of bodily assistance in this thy ordinary *creature*, and prosper thy meanes of spirituall assistance in thy holy *Ordinances*."[167] He returns, however, in the Thirteenth Prayer, to the idea of God sending the sickness for correction and more specifically now for purification. His sickness is the vehicle for coming to God. "These heates, *O Lord*, which thou hast broght upon this *body*, are but thy chafing of the *wax*, that thou mightest *seale* me to thee."[168] And in the Fifteenth Expostulation, sickness is referred to as God's physic, the treatment he uses to bring Donne to him. "Since the whole sicknesse is thy *Physicke*, shall any accident in it, bee my poison, by my murmuring?"[169]

Donne's Need for Relationship with God

Lighten our darkness, we beseech thee, O Lord; and by thy great mercy defend us from all perils and dangers of this night; for the love of thy only Son, our Saviour, Jesus Christ. Amen.

—THE BOOK OF COMMON PRAYER[170]

Although Donne responds to God in his time of emotional and physical upheaval as a savior and also as the instigator of his disease, there is another image which continues to appear in the *Devotions*. That is, the God who Donne fears will withdraw his relationship. He does not say "has" withdrawn, a thought which is too threatening theologically. However, when the relationship is reestablished in the acceptance section, it is apparent that this union has not been experienced earlier and that the earlier relationship was seen in terms of stability rather than interaction. The fear of loss of relationship with God appears very early in the book. In the Second Prayer, he asks

---

167. Donne, *Devotions* (Sparrow), 73.
168. Donne, *Devotions* (Sparrow), 78.
169. Donne, *Devotions* (Sparrow), 89.
170. *Book of Common Prayer*, 70.

for assurance that God is still there, that he has not withdrawn from him in this time of need. "And, *O my God*, who madest thyself a *Light* in a *Bush*, in the middest of these *brambles*, and *thornes* of a sharpe sicknesse, appeare unto me so, that I may see thee, and know thee to be my *God*, applying thy selfe to me, even in these sharp, and thorny passages."[171] In the Third Prayer, Donne again displays his need for a relationship with God in his illness, by asserting that this relationship is still intact. The prayer begins "O Most mightie and most merciful *God*, who though thou have taken me off of my feet, hast not taken me off of my foundation, which is *thy selfe*."[172] Donne then names different ways that he can still be in touch with God:

1. as contemplator—"though thou have removed me from that upright forme, in which I could stand, and see thy throne, the *Heavens*, yet hast not removed from mee that light, by which I can lie and see thy selfe;"[173]

2. as worshipper—"who, though thou have weakened my bodily knees, that they cannot bow to thee, hast yet left mee the knees of my heart, which are bowed unto thee evermore;"[174]

3. as sacrifice—"As thou hast made this *bed*, thine *Altar*, make me thy *Sacrifice*;"[175] and

4. as priest—"as thou makest thy *Sonne Christ Jesus* the *Priest*, so make me his *Deacon*, to minister to him in a chereful surrender of my body, and soule to thy pleasure, by his hands."[176]

That this is a theological enumeration of various relationships possible with God, rather than an affirmation of Donne's own relationship is obvious from the great agitation of Donne's feelings, in these expostulations and prayers; by his excessive reiteration of his need for an ongoing relationship with God, a relationship that has not changed, that will give stability to the chaos that is his illness. He cannot admit openly to his feelings of estrangement from God, except to ask for assurances of his presence.

Expostulation V again verbalizes Donne's need for relationship with God. "I am not able to passe this agony alone; not alone without *thee*; Thou art thy spirit; not alone without *thine*; spirituall and temporall *Phisicians*, are

171. Donne, *Devotions* (Sparrow), 10.
172. Donne, *Devotions* (Sparrow), 14.
173. Donne, *Devotions* (Sparrow), 14.
174. Donne, *Devotions* (Sparrow), 14.
175. Donne, *Devotions* (Sparrow), 14.
176. Donne, *Devotions* (Sparrow), 14.

thine; not alone without *mine*; Those whom the bands of *blood* or *friendship*, hath made *mine*, are *mine*; And if *thou*, or *thine*, or *mine*, abandon me, I am alone, and woe unto me, if I bee alone."[177] And although Expostulation VI states his theological knowledge that "*God* is never asleep nor absent,"[178] in the Thirteenth Prayer, the need for assurance of God's presence with him is again verbalized. "Onley be thou ever present to me, *O my God*, and this *bed–chamber*, and thy bed–chamber shal be all one roome, and the closing of these bodily *Eyes* here, and the opening of the *Eyes* of my *Soule*, there, all one *Act*."[179] The Fourteenth Prayer asks God directly not to leave him:

> Let thy mercifull providence so governe all in this *sicknesse*, that I never fall into utter *darknesse, ignorance of thee*, or *inconsideration of myselfe*; and let those *shadowes* which doe fall upon mee, *faintnesses of Spirit*, and *condemnations of my selfe*, bee overcome by the power of thine irresistible *light*, the *God of consolation*; that when those *shadowes* have done their office upon mee, to let me see, that of my selfe I should fall into irrecoverable darknesse, thy *spirit* may doe his *office* upon those *shadowes*, and disperse them . . . and that the words of thy *Sonne*, spoken to his *Apostles*, may reflect upon me, *Behold, I am with you alwaies, even to the end of the world*.[180]

Thus Donne, in his Expostulations and Prayers which occur before he hears the passing bell, describes the powerfulness of God in two different aspects. He hopes that God the divine Physician, will save him from his illness either directly, or through his physician; and that He will protect him from bad doctors. He also sees the sickness, itself, as being sent by God, either as a sign of anger, or as a correction, which involves a purgation of past sins, and purification for the anticipated future life with God. In response to seeing sickness as God's means of correction, Donne feels the need to submit to God's plan. He is, however, not able to achieve this submission, regardless of his avowed conscious desire to obey God's will, while he is still emotionally and physically rejecting his illness.

Coexistent with these ideas of God is the fear that God will withdraw himself from relationship with Donne during this period of great stress and leave him alone to experience death. The desperate need for continuing relationship has been seen to be expressed by Donne throughout these exercises. It is at this point in his meditations that Donne's empathy with

177. Donne, *Devotions* (Sparrow), 25.
178. Donne, *Devotions* (Sparrow), 30.
179. Donne, *Devotions* (Sparrow), 78.
180. Donne, *Devotions* (Sparrow), 86.

his dying neighbor is described and that empathy marks his acceptance of his own situation. A parallel development occurs in the expostulations and prayers during this period.

In Expostulation XVI, Donne asks God why he has bells rung at funerals because the person whose funeral it is will not need them. "But he for whose funerall these *Bells* ring now, was at *home*, at his journies end, *yesterday*; why ring they now?"[181] He observes that if they are sent to remind him of his death they are superfluous because he already has enough reminders in his own physical condition. And yet, not really superfluous, because they are aids to better understanding God:

> Neither doest thou only doe good to us all, in *life* and *death*, but also wouldest have us doe good to one another, as in a holy *life*, so in those things which accompanie our *death*: In that Contemplation I make account that I heare this dead brother of ours, who is now carried out to his *buriall*, to speake to mee, and to preach my *Funerall Sermon*, in the voice of these *Bells*. In him, O *God*, thou hast accomplished to mee, even the request of *Dives* to *Abraham*; *Thou hast sent one from the dead to speake unto mee*. He speakes to mee aloud from that *Steeple*; hee whispers to mee at these *Curtaines*, and hee speaks thy words; *Blessed are the dead which die in the Lord, from henceforth.*[182]

This Expostulation and Prayer are significant from several different aspects. First, it marks a change from Donne's introspective examination of his sickness and its meaning in relationship to an all-powerful God. Secondly, it marks Donne's first verbalization that a relationship with God involves relationship with other men—that sharing is a part of experiencing God. Third, it marks the point where Donne is able to accept without fear, the help of other men, and finally, in continuing the discussion of the bells directly into the expostulation, it lowers the formal barriers between secular and religious experience.

This new ability to receive aid from others parallels Donne's ability in Expostulation and Prayer XVII to accept aid from God, not through a controlled acceptance or submission, but by Donne becoming able to receive God in suffering. This is not achieved without struggle, however; for Donne, who recognizes the message of the bells for him, still protests against suffering as a means of growth:

---

181. Donne, *Devotions* (Sparrow), 94.
182. Donne, *Devotions* (Sparrow), 96.

> My *God*, my *God*, is this one of thy waies, of *drawing light out of darknesse*, to make *him* for whom this *bell* tolls, now in this dimnesse of his sight, to become a *superintendent*, an *overseer*, a *Bishop*, to as many as heare his *voice*, in this *bell*, and to give us a *confirmation* in this action? Is this one of thy waies *to raise strength out of weaknesse*, to make him who cannot rise *from his bed*, nor stirre *in his bed*, come *home* to *me*, and in this sound, give mee the strength of *healthy* and vigorous *instructions*? . . . But, O my *God*, my *God*, since *heaven* is *glory* and *joy*, why doe not *glorious* and *joyfull* things lead us, induce us to *heaven*? . . . Why hast thou changed thine old way, and carried us by the waies of *discipline* and *mortification*, by the waies of *mourning* and *lamentation*, by the waies of *miserable ends*, and *miserable anticipations* of those miseries, in appropriating the *exemplar* miseries of others to our selves, and *usurping* upon their *miseries*, as our owne, to our owne *prejudice*?[183]

The expostulation ends, however, with an affirmation by Donne that he is experiencing joy and glory even in his affliction, and that his distress is not a foil to future joy, but contains joy and glory itself. "Pardon, O *God*, this *unthankfull rashnesse*; I that aske why thou *doest not*, finde even now in *my selfe*, that thou *doest*; such *joy*, such *glory*, as that I conclude upon *my selfe*, upon *all*, They that finde not *joy* in their *sorrowes*, *glory* in their dejections in this *world*, are in fearefull *danger* of missing both in the *next*."[184]

Donne's thought expression suffers here through his use of seventeenth-century theological language as a vehicle for communicating his experience. This also applies to the prayer which ends the devotion, in which Donne verbalizes his acceptance, not only in theological language; but in terms by which he has previously asserted his desire to submit to God's will: "I humbly accept thy *voice* in the sound of this sad and funerall *bell*. And first, I blesse thy glorious name, that in this *sound* and *voice* I can hear thy *instructions*, in *another mans* to consider *mine owne condition*; and to know, that this *Bell* which *tolls* for another, before it come to *ring out*, may take in me too . . . therefore, *into thy hands*, O my *God*, *I commend my spirit*; A *surrender*, which I know thou wilt accept, whether I *live* or *die*."[185]

A comparison of this passage, however, to the former avowals of surrender, quickly shows that Donne is not reiterating earlier speeches. In Prayer VI, Donne prays "let me feele [these fears] to determine, where his

---

183. Donne, *Devotions* (Sparrow), 98–100.
184. Donne, *Devotions* (Sparrow), 100.
185. Donne, *Devotions* (Sparrow), 101.

feare did, in a present submitting of all to thy will."[186] Later in Prayer VII, he prays for God "to make this correction . . . to tast so to me, not as I would, but as thou wouldest have it taste, and to conform my tast, and make it agreeable to thy will."[187] And in Prayer XI, he states that "*Infirmitie of Nature, Curiositie of Minde*, are tentations that offer; but a silent, and absolute obedience, to thy will, even before I know it, is my *Cordiall*."[188]

In each of these earlier prayers, Donne is speaking of altering his thoughts and emotions to conform with God's will through an act of will on his part. In this Seventeenth Prayer, however, he is, as Christ did, commending his spirit into God's hands. This is not imposing a pattern on himself that he cannot emotionally or physically accept, but rather, trusting his spirit, his mind and emotions, to that ultimacy which he recognizes structures and gives meaning to life. This interpretation is further strengthened by his reiteration of his acceptance of ultimacy. "Declare thou thy will upon mee, O *Lord*, for *life* or *death*, in thy time; receive my *surrender* of my selfe, now, *Into thy hands, O Lord, I commend my spirit.*"[189] Donne is not giving up his ideas, or his hopes, or his fears. He is placing himself, as he is, within that order that he perceives to be ultimacy. He is accepting his place in that structure, and trusting, commending that which makes him human, his spirit, to that perceived order. He has not been able to do this before, because he was still adjusting to a milieu oriented to sick role behavior, and grieving for his old environment in which his independence and control over his health had created the illusion that he could control his life and dictate the pattern of which he was a part. Now, having worked through his grief over losing his old order, he is able to see himself in perspective, in a relationship to cosmic order, and commit himself to this framework.

Then, having regained his orientation, he can stop concentrating on his own survival and act as a human being in response to the need of the dying parishioner. "And being thus, O my *God*, prepared by thy *correction*, mellowed by thy chastisement, and conformed to thy will, by thy *Spirit*, having received thy *pardon* for my *Soule*, and asking no *reprieve* for my *Body*, I am bold, O Lord, to bend my *prayers* to thee, for his *assistance*, the voice of whose *bell* hath called mee to this *devotion*."[190] There then follows an intercession for the dying man, in which Donne prays for God to be with this person and to make Him aware of His presence as he leaves this world. It

186. Donne, *Devotions* (Sparrow), 34.
187. Donne, *Devotions* (Sparrow), 40.
188. Donne, *Devotions* (Sparrow), 67.
189. Donne, *Devotions* (Sparrow), 101.
190. Donne, *Devotions* (Sparrow), 101.

verbalizes and projects Donne's old fear of loss of relationship with God, a fear which has been acknowledged by him from the early stage of his illness; which is another dimension from his projections of God as savior and disciplinary judge.

Expostulations and Prayers XVI–XVIII, however, do not present any continuation of Donne's pleas for assurance of God's presence. Donne experiences God through the passing bell and funeral bell of the parishioner, and is so certain that God is choosing this means to communicate with him that he displays none of the old misery over the idea of separation that appears earlier in the *Devotions*. In experiencing communion with God through the suffering of others, he achieves that assurance of God's presence which he has agonized over before. In this prayer he asks God to remain with the dying man, in his transition from earth to heaven:

> When thy *Sonne* cried out upon the *Crosse, My God, my God, Why hast thou forsaken me?* he spake not so much in his *owne Person*, as in the person of the *Church*, and of his afflicted *members*, who in deep distresses might feare thy *forsaking*. This *patient*, O most blessed *God*, is one of *them*; in his behalfe, and in his name, heare thy *Sonne* crying to thee, *My God, my God, why hast thou forsaken me?* and forsake him not; but with thy *left hand* lay his *body* in the *grave* . . . and with thy *right hand* receive his *soule* into thy *Kingdome*, and unite *him* and *us* in one *Communion of Saints*. Amen.[191]

The prayer for the dying man thus formally lays to rest those fears of isolation from God that Donne has previously experienced, but which are no longer relevant to him, now that he is apprehending that all-inclusive order that is God, and experiencing this order in the ministration of the bells to him and in his reciprocal intercession for the man for whom the bell tolled.

The third part of this acceptance section of the *Devotions* continues the contemplation of mortality, this time in relationship to the funeral bell. In Expostulation XVIII, Donne notes again the interrelationship of men's woes which he finds illustrated in the help the dead man's bell has given him. "Is not this, O my God, a holy kinde of *raising up seed to my dead brother*, if I, by the meditation of his *death*, produce a better *life* in my selfe?"[192] He is not concerned with his old behavior, which he believes to be forgiven, and he defines sin for himself now as not being responsive to that state of awareness into which he has entered by means of the bells: "If the death of this man worke not upon mee now, I shall die worse, than if thou hadst not

191. Donne, *Devotions* (Sparrow), 102.
192. Donne, *Devotions* (Sparrow), 107.

afforded me this helpe: for thou hast sent *him* in this *Bell* to mee, as thou didst send to the *Angell of Sardis*, with *commission to strengthen the things that remaine, and that are ready to die*; that in this weaknes of *body*, I might receive spiritual strength, by these occasions."[193] He concludes this expostulation with a strong statement of what happens to a person who shuts out his awareness gained by shared suffering. "May not the neglecting of this *sound* ministred to mee in this *mans death*, bring mee to that miserie, as that I, whom the *Lord of life* loved so, as to die for me, shall *die*, and a *Creature* of mine owne shall be *immortall*; that I shall die, and the *worme of mine owne conscience* shall never die?"[194] This is a strong expression, of the state of a person who has, through hardness of heart, knowingly refused to interact and grow through human interaction, and who ceases to be truly human by this refusal, experiences death of the spirit and continues to exist, filled with the torment of his own refusal. In this statement of sin, Donne demonstrates a new awareness of his responsibilities as a human being to other humans that rises above the catalogue of personal indiscretions that has previously haunted him.

This devotion closes once again with a prayer for the dying man, within the larger prayer of Donne to God. "Whether this voice *instruct* mee, that I am a *dead man* now, or *remember* me, that I have been a *dead man* all this while, I humbly thanke thee for speaking in this *voice* to my *soule*, and I humbly beseech thee also, to accept my prayers in his behalfe, by whose occasion this *voice*, this *sound* is come to mee."[195] The prayer is specifically for the speedy reunion of the man's soul with his body in heaven. From this petition, however, Donne moves on to a holistic vision of Christ's second coming in which all just souls will be actualized in their bodies, in which sin will be abolished and all manifestations of sin gone, and in which the elect will participate eternally in complete relationship with God:

> That that blessed *Sonne* of thine, may have the *consummation* of his *dignitie*, by entring into his *last office*, the office of a *Judge*, and may have *societie* of humane *bodies* in *heaven*, as well as he hath had ever of *soules*; And that as thou hatest *sinne* it selfe, thy *hate* to *sinne* may bee expressed in the abolishing of all *instruments of sin*, The *allurements* of this *world*, and the *world* it selfe; and all the *temporarie revenges* of sinne, the *stings* of *sicknesse* and of *death*; and all the *castles*, and *prisons*, and *monuments* of *sinne*, in the *grave*. That *time* may bee swallowed up in

---

193. Donne, *Devotions* (Sparrow), 107.
194. Donne, *Devotions* (Sparrow), 108.
195. Donne, *Devotions* (Sparrow), 109.

Eternitie, and *hope* swallowed in *possession*, and *ends* swallowed in *infinitenesse*, and *all men* ordained to *salvation*, in *body* and *soule* be *one intire* and *everlasting sacrifice* to thee, where thou mayest receive *delight* from them, and they *glorie* from thee, for evermore. *Amen.*[196]

It is a rose vision, in which Donne portrays that everlasting reciprocation of delight that is experienced in moments out of time. In this apprehension of consummation, Donne includes sickness and death, as part of the temporary ravages of sin—they exist in the order that is God but are not seen here as being sent by God. This also marks an advance of Donne's awareness, from seeing sickness and death as instruments of God's discipline, he moves to seeing them as existing within God's order now, but not partaking of God's essence. He eliminates them from the final consummation of joy, just as he eliminates "all the *castles*, and *prisons*, and *monuments* of *sinne*."[197] The imagery is significant, calling up Donne's own experience with and distaste for imprisonment. Thus, although Donne defines sin in conventional religious terminology, his examples of sin's expression—sickness and death—and his choice of images for sin are very personal revelations of those things that Donne had trouble dealing with in his own life. And finally, in his vision of the consummation of Christ's kingdom, he lays to rest the problems of change which he cries out against in these *Devotions*. Time is "swallowed up in *Eternitie*," hope is swallowed in possession, ends swallowed in infiniteness, and body and soul exist forever in an eternal relationship with God.[198] Dante, in his final Canto of *Paradise* in the *Divine Comedy*, also describes an experience of merging with God.

---

196. Donne, *Devotions* (Sparrow), 110.
197. Donne, *Devotions* (Sparrow), 110.
198. Donne, *Devotions* (Sparrow), 110.

Divine Comedy: **Paradise: Canto XXXIII**

O Light Eternal, that sole abides in Thyself, sole understandest Thyself, and by Thyself understood and understanding, lovest and smilest on Thyself! That circle, which appeared in Thee generated as a reflected light, being awhile surveyed by my eyes, seemed to me depicted with our effigy within itself, of its own very color; wherefore my sight was wholly set upon it. As is the geometer who wholly applies himself to measure the circle, and finds not by thinking that principle of which he is in need, such was I at that new sight. I wished to see how the image was conformed to the circle, and how it has its place therein; but my own wings were not for this, had it not been that my mind was smitten by a flash in which its wish came.

To the high fantasy here power failed; but now my desire and my will were revolved, like a wheel which is moved evenly, by the Love which moves the sun and the other stars.[199]

---

199. Alighieri, *Divine Comedy*, ll. 124–45.

After this eternal moment of union with God, in whom God the Savior and Judge is consumed in the ultimacy of God who is all in all, and in whom Donne's relationship to God has been reestablished, extending the sharing of human needs to the sharing of divine order, it is interesting to pick up Donne's Expostulations once more and follow the use he makes of his awareness as he enters convalescence.

In Expostulation XIX, his integration is expressed, as in the Meditation that precedes it, by his affirmation of his belief in the ability of the doctor to help him. He uses an extended analogy of the doctors as ships sent from God to help him over the sea of illness. He thus accepts the order to which he has committed himself, and is able to trust those appointed to help him within that order. This new trust is expressed within the old framework of writing. Donne uses analogies to extend the discussion of a subject begun in the Meditation to a spiritual dimension in the Expostulations. This is the form he uses most often before his acceptance, and it is not discarded now. Just as in the analysis of the Meditations it was observed that Donne's frame of behavior does not change after his adjustment to his illness, this is now true of his method of relating to God. Having established a relationship once more, that relationship is expressed within the old forms. The ultimate concern secure, Donne returns to a dialogue with the various views of God that he needs. Within the positive view of the outcome of his illness, Donne talks with God as Savior, "though thou have beene pleased to *glorifie* thy selfe in a long exercise of my *patience*, with an *expectation* of thy *declaration* of thy selfe in this my *sicknesse*, yet since thou hast now of thy goodnesse afforded that, which affords us some hope, if that bee still *the way* of thy *glory*, proceed in *that way*, and perfit *that worke*, and establish me in a *Sabbath*, and *rest* in *thee*, by this thy *seale* of *bodily restitution*."[200]

He is also concerned again with maintaining his relationship with God. "If thou shouldest take thy *hand* utterly from me, and have nothing to doe with me, *nature* alone were able to *destroy* me."[201] Once again Donne's old patterns are at work. A lifetime of insecurity and survival within a hostile system cannot be so easily thrown over, and even as he experiences the new order of heightened awareness of God, he continues to experience his old insecurities within this order; and he asks for reassurance of the relationship. But although old behavior persists, it is less severe, less urgent, than at the beginning of the *Devotions*.

---

200. Donne, *Devotions* (Sparrow), 118.
201. Donne, *Devotions* (Sparrow), 119.

In Expostulation XX, God is addressed as "the *God* of *Order*," and this feeling of orientation overrides the continued fears of losing God again.[202] This order is expressed through one of Donne's favorite images—the compass: "As hee that would describe a *circle* in paper, if hee have brought that *circle* within one *inch* of *finishing*, yet if he remove his *compasse*, he cannot make it up a perfit *circle*, except he fall to worke againe, to finde out the same *center*, so, though setting that *foot* of my *compasse* upon *thee*, I have gone so farre, as to the *consideration* of my selfe, yet if I depart from *thee*, my *center*, all is unperfit."[203] Donne seeks, in terms of spiritual analogies to purge himself of his past sins, through confession, in order to maintain this God centered relationship.

In Prayer XXII, which ends the devotion on physical and spiritual eradication of disease, Donne addresses God as "the *God* of *securitie*, and the *enemie* of *securitie* too, who wouldest have us alwaies *sure* of thy *love*, and yet wouldest have us alwaies *doing something* for it," and petitions him to "let mee alwaies so apprehend thee, as *present* with me, and yet so *follow* after thee, as though I had not apprehended thee."[204] This is a request for God to help Donne to remain secure in God's order without losing his enthusiasm for action within that order; a request for maintenance of relationship that includes growth within that relationship and precludes the inactivity of self-satisfaction.

Finally, Expostulation XXIII continues the use of analogies to express Donne's fear of spiritual relapse, just as he fears physical relapse. He is terrified of losing forever his communion with God through his inability to maintain his relationship and ends Prayer XXIII with a plea for God to not forsake him, if he should do something that would disturb this state. And so, it is with Donne fearful of losing his new established order that the *Devotions* end. This Donne, who anticipates all eventualities and attempts to prepare for them, is ostensibly the same as Donne who cries out in the first Meditation when an external event disrupts his carefully planned order. Yet, despite the old mechanisms which respond to the old fears, change has occurred. Physical and emotional upheaval have been worked through to a perception of God that includes shared suffering. The experience of union with God does not recede leaving Donne the same person as before, despite the fact that he continues old behavior patterns and old anxieties. Although his desire for relationship remains consistent, it is a different type of

---

202. Donne, *Devotions* (Sparrow), 122.
203. Donne, *Devotions* (Sparrow), 123–24.
204. Donne, *Devotions* (Sparrow), 138.

relationship from that of approval or disapproval sought in the beginning; it is union with God that is experienced, not a contractual arrangement.

Having acknowledged that this experience occurs, it is also necessary to recognize that Donne's trust level still remains low, that it continues to be difficult for him to remain empathetically open to others, and that he thus slips quickly from a state of union, emotionally and physically experienced, into his old familiar pattern of union, intellectually perceived and mentally desired, but emotionally blocked by his own lack of trust and inability to relinquish control. It is a goal to be worked for, or a moment out of time experienced after much stress, rather than a way of traveling for him.

An examination of Donne's life proves helpful in understanding the difficulty that he experiences with openness and in perhaps clarifying the need to control that he exhibits both in his response to change and in his relationship to God.

Donne's Life: In Search of Order

And new Philosophy calls all in doubt,
The Element of fire is quite put out;
The Sun is lost, and th'earth, and no mans wit
Can well direct him where to looke for it.
And freely men confesse that this world's spent,
When in the Planets, and the Firmament
They seeke so many new; then see that this
Is crumbled out againe to his Atomies.
'Tis all in peeces, all cohaerence gone;
All just supply, and all Relation:
Prince, Subject, Father, Sonne, are things forgot,
For every man alone thinkes he hath got,
To be a Phoenix, and that then can bee
None of that kinde, of which he is, but hee.
This is the worlds condition now.
— An Anatomie of the World, John Donne, 1611–12[205]

---

205. Coffin, *Complete Poetry*, 191.

John Donne was born in London on Bread Street in 1572.[206] His father was a prosperous member of the Worshipful Company of Ironmongers, who Isaac Walton says was of Welsh descent.[207] In 1573, he became Warden of that Company. Donne's mother, Elizabeth Heywood, was a relative of Sir Thomas More, who had been Lord Chancellor of England under Henry VIII.[208] When Donne was four years old, his father died, leaving a substantial estate to his children. As only two of them survived into adult life, Donne inherited a more than adequate sum when he came of age. His mother remarried shortly after his father's death; this time to Dr. John Syminges, a physician who, Bald states, had several times been President of the Royal College of Physicians. Donne lived in that household until he was sent to Oxford University in 1584 when he was eleven years old. He remained there, in Hart Hall, until he was fourteen, at which time he left Oxford without a degree and it is said that he entered Cambridge, staying there until he was seventeen. Coffin states that "he received a degree from neither university because he could not take the oath required at graduation."[209]

The household of Dr. Syminges was Roman Catholic. Donne's mother's family, the Heywoods, with its connection to that of Sir Thomas More, was active in the effort to gain political toleration for Roman Catholics in England. His uncle, Jasper Heywood, who had been educated at Oxford, was trained on the continent to be a Jesuit priest and was among the first Jesuits to come to England for missionary purposes. After successfully laying a foundation for Roman Catholic coordination in England, this same uncle was apprehended by the English authorities as he was attempting to leave the country and was imprisoned in the Tower of London. It is assumed that Donne's mother visited him there and that Donne himself knew of these meetings. Certainly, he was aware from early childhood of the persecution of Roman Catholic Englishmen and of the efforts of the more zealous Roman Catholics for an alleviation of these inequities. He refers to this experience in the preface to his work on suicide entitled *Bianthantos*. "I had my first breeding and conversation with men of suppressed and afflicted Religion, accustomed to the despite of death, and hungry of an imagin'd martyrdome."[210] Again, in referring to his later change to the Anglican Church of England he states:

> I used no inordinate hast, nor precipatation in binding my conscience to any local Religion. I had a longer worke to doe than

---

206. Bald, *John Donne*, 35.
207. See Appendix 4 on the Ironmongers and John Donne's father.
208. See Appendix 3 on John Donne's mother.
209. Coffin, *Complete Poetry*, xxii.
210. Coffin, *Complete Poetry*, 303.

many other men; for I was first to blot out, certain impressions of the Roman Religion, and to wrestle both against the examples and against the reasons by which some hold was taken; and some anticipations early layde upon my conscience, both by Persons who by nature had a power and superiority over my will, and others who by their learning and good life, seem'd to me justly to claime an interest for the guiding and rectifying of mine understanding in these matters.[211]

The underground activities of English Roman Catholics and their persecution which was seen first hand in the life of Donne's uncle was to come even closer to Donne. In 1593, while he and his brother Henry were in London, John at Lincoln's Inn and Henry at Thavies Inn, a priest named William Harrington sought shelter in Henry's chambers. While there, he was discovered by the officials, was subsequently imprisoned, and despite protestations of innocence of subversive activity, was sentenced to be hanged, drawn, and quartered. Donne's brother was also imprisoned in Newgate for offering his rooms as lodging to Harrington, and while he was in prison, he contracted the plague from his fellow inmates and was dead within a few days. Here again, religious dissent had resulted in imprisonment, this time followed by death itself, for a member of Donne's immediate family.

Donne's family suffered physically for their faith by imprisonment and death. They also suffered financially. When John Heywood, Donne's mother's cousin, was declared a recusant by refusing to sign the Oath of Allegiance, "under the penalties imposed by the Act of 1587 two-thirds of his lands became forfeited to the Crown."[212] John Donne himself was given the administration of these lands. A second incidence of financial deprivation experienced by Donne's family involves Richard Rainsford, third husband of Donne's mother. "Rainsford had been convicted for refusal to take the Oath of Allegiance, and conviction for this offence entailed the penalties of praemunire: loss of the King's protection, loss of property, and imprisonment during the King's pleasure."[213] Rainsford was subsequently imprisoned in Newgate for several years and suffered loss of property.

These events which involve financial loss as well as imprisonment within one extended family are illustrative of the type of deprivation experienced by those Englishmen who continued to adhere to the old religion. Another form of religious persecution that was directly related to Donne's life was the fact that Roman Catholics could not be awarded degrees from

---

211. Coffin, *Complete Poetry*, 313–14.
212. Bald, *John Donne*, 116.
213. Bald, *John Donne*, 267.

the universities unless they took an oath "acknowledging the royal supremacy in matters of religion."[214] Donne entered Oxford before he was of an age to be required to take this oath and he left Oxford without a degree.

These incidents give some idea of the extent to which Donne knew religious persecution in his formative years. They do not, however, indicate the day-to-day experience of growing up apart from the predominant culture of a country. Instead of participating in the nationalism of the English Renaissance, it may be postulated that the sub-group of Roman Catholics who continued to live in England found their support among their own people and viewed the activities of the government from a detached and often critical viewpoint.[215] Being a member of a persecuted minority would call for guarded speech and a sensitivity to the threat of danger that would warn of approaching persecution. The environment, then, in which Donne spent his youth, was one which could easily have nurtured feelings of minority superiority and would have taught caution and survival skills through day-to-day behavior patterns.

When Donne went to London to study law at Lincoln's Inn, he was soon to be in possession of a generous inheritance from his father. At the death of his brother, only two children—John and his sister Anne—remained from the original family of six who were living when the elder Donne died, and the inheritance was divided between them. Donne had received approximately seven hundred and fifty pounds by 1594, with which he proceeded to live in the style of a young courtier.[216] A miniature painted at this time reveals a taste for clothes. We know that he traveled in Europe during this period, also, and that in 1596 he went with Robert Devereux, the Second Earl of Essex on an expedition to Cadiz, Spain that resulted in the capture of the city by the English, and the destruction of much of the Spanish fleet. He signed on to this venture as Gentleman. After returning to England for a time, Donne again went with Essex and Sir Walter Raleigh on another expedition which ended up in the Azores, with less success than before. It was on the second voyage that Donne met the son of the Lord Keeper, Sir Thomas Egerton. Upon Donne's return, he was appointed secretary to the Lord Keeper himself in 1597, and he began a career that promised to blossom into work at high diplomatic levels. Donne was imminently qualified for this type of work by his education, background, and travel. He apparently moved easily with the court set and developed life-long friendships during this period. In 1601, he entered Parliament as a member for Brackly

---

214. Bald, *John Donne*, 42.
215. Hunt, *Donne's Poetry*, 170.
216. Walton says it was 3,000 pounds, not 750. Bald, *John Donne*, 57.

(October–December). Walton ends his *Life of Dr. John Donne* with a description of him that seems appropriate here:

> He was of stature moderately tall; of a straight and equally proportioned body, to which all his words and actions gave an inexpressible addition of comeliness.
>
> The melancholy and pleasant humor were in him so contempered, that each gave advantage to the other, and made his company one of the delights of mankind.
>
> His fancy was inimitably high, equaled only by his great wit; both being made useful by a commanding judgment.
>
> His aspect was cheerful, and such as gave a silent testimony of a clear knowing soul, and of a conscience at peace with itself.
>
> His melting eye showed that he had a soft heart, full of noble compassion; of too brave a soul to offer injuries, and too much a Christian not to pardon them in others.
>
> He did much contemplate—especially after he entered into his sacred calling—the mercies of Almighty God, the immortality of the soul, and the joys of heaven: and would often say in a kind of sacred ecstasy—Blessed be 'God that He is God, only and divinely like Himself.'
>
> He was by nature highly passionate, but more apt to reluct at the excesses of it. A great lover of the offices of humanity, and of so merciful a spirit that he never beheld the miseries of mankind without pity and relief.
>
> He was earnest and unwearied in the search of knowledge, with which his vigorous soul is now satisfied, and employed in a continual praise of that God that first breathed it into his active body: that body which once was a temple of the Holy Ghost, and is now become a small quantity of Christian dust:
>
> —But I shall see it reanimated.[217]

---

217. Walton, *Lives of Donne and Herbert*, l–li.

Goe and Catch a Falling Star (Song)

Goe and catche a falling starre,
    Get with child a mandrake roote,
Tell me where all past yeares are,
    Or who cleft the Divels foot,
Teach me to heare Mermaides singing,
    Or to keep off envies stinging,
        And finde
        What winde
Serves to advance an honest minde.

If thou beest borne to strange sights,
    Things invisible to see,
Ride ten thousand daies and nights,
    Till age snow white haires on thee,
Thou, when thou retorn'st, wilt tell mee,
All strange wonders that befell thee,
        And sweare,
        No where
Lives a woman true, and faire.

If thou findst one, let mee know,
    Such a Pilgrimage were sweet;
Yet doe not, I would not goe,
    Though at next doore wee might meet;
Though shee were true, when you met her,
    And last, till you write your letter,
        Yet shee
        Will bee
False, ere I come, to two, or three.

JOHN DONNE, PRIOR TO 1601[218]

---

218. Grierson, *Metaphysical*, 2.

With all signs favorable for a distinguished career, Donne fell in love with Ann More, a niece of Sir Thomas Egerton's wife. Ann's father was Sir George More who was then Chancellor of the Garter and Lieutenant of the Tower. She was a girl who was of too high a social standing to marry him. Donne, however, with full awareness of the imprudence of the match, pressed his suit, and was married to Ann just before Christmas 1601, without her father's knowledge or permission. Elopement was a serious act in the seventeenth century. Property was a determining factor in alliances within great families, and marriage contracts were arranged by parents. The flouting of convention and the impecunity of Donne (who had already spent his inheritance) combined to anger Sir George More so much when he eventually learned of the marriage on February 2, 1602, that he had Donne thrown into one prison and the priest who married them, Samuel Brooke, into another. He also prevailed on Sir Thomas Egerton to dismiss Donne, and although More afterwards repented of his haste and had Donne released from prison, he was never able to persuade Egerton to rehire Donne. Egerton stated: "Though he was unfeignedly sorry for what he had done, yet it was inconsistent with his place and credit, to discharge and readmit servants at the request of passionate petitioners."[219]

Donne's dismissal from Egerton marked the real end of his diplomatic career, although Donne continued to seek preferment at court for the next ten years. During this period, Donne's life fell into a pattern of seeking financial support for his growing family from his old friends and from patrons for whom he wrote. At first, he lived for a time with his friend and Ann's cousin Sir Francis Wolley at Pyrford. Then, after Wolley's death, Donne traveled on the continent with Chute. He moved in 1606 to a house in the country outside London at Mitcham. During those years, in addition to Wolley, Sir Henry Goodyer, Lucy, Countess of Bedford, and Mrs. Magdalene Herbert were among Donne's patrons. He wrote poems to them and carried on a weekly correspondence with Goodyer that is an important source of information on Donne's activities.

It was in this period after his marriage, and before his friendship with Sir Robert Drury, that Donne assisted Thomas Morton, who was to become the Bishop of Durham, in writing arguments refuting Jesuit positions. The result of the collaboration with Morton was more far reaching than the publication of religious tracts. Morton was so impressed with Donne's expertise that he tried to persuade him to enter the church at that time. Donne, still hopeful of secular advancement, continued to refuse to take holy orders. His tract writing led, however, to the composition of *Pseudo–Martyr*, which was published in 1610. Coffin says that "*Pseudo–Martyr* defends the proposition

---

219. Walton, *Lives of Donne and Herbert*, xii.

that 'those which are of the Romane Religion in this Kingdome, may and ought to take the Oath of Allegiance,' and condemns, as unwarranted self-persecution and 'false martyrdom,' the reward of martyrdom which the Jesuits promised to their followers who might suffer death for refusing to take the Oath."[220] It was written in response to the Catholic distress over being required by James I to take the Oath of Allegiance in the aftermath of the Gunpowder Plot. It was in nature conciliatory, as its objective was to persuade Roman Catholics to take the oath. This work raised Donne's reputation in England but instead of procuring him a court position, it moved the King, Walton says, to persuade Donne to enter the ministry; a step he still refused to take. Following the book's publication in 1610, Donne wrote a satire on the Jesuits called *Ignatius, His Conclave*. This was published anonymously in 1611 and was a strong attack on the activities of that order.

A third book that was written during the years Donne spent at Mitcham with his family is *Biathanatos*, a treatise that argues the possibility of suicide not being always a sin. This treatise was written in 1608, but not published until 1646, many years after Donne's death. That Donne would choose to write on suicide seems to reflect his own melancholia during these hard years. This melancholia is evident in his letters to Goodyer:

> (Mitcham, c. 1608).
> ... The pleasantnesse of the season displeases me. Every thing refreshes, and I wither, and I grow older and not better, my strength diminishes, and my load growes, and being to passe more and more stormes, I finde that I have not only cast out all my ballast which nature and time gives, Reason and discretion, and so am as empty and light as Vanity can make me; but I have over fraught my selfe with Vice, and so am ridd[l]ingly subject to two contrary wrackes, Sinking and Oversetting, and under the iniquity of such a disease as inforces the patient when he is almost starved, not only to fast but to purge.[221]

> Sir, (Mitcham, Sept, 1608)
> Every tuesday I make account that I turn a great hourglass and consider that a weeks life is run out since I writ. But if I ask myself what I have done in the last watch, or would do in the next, I can say nothing; if I say that I have passed it without hurting any, so may the Spider in my window... Two of the most precious things which God hath afforded us here, for the agony and exercise of our sense and spirit, which are a thirst and inhiation after the next life, and a

---

220. Coffin, *Complete Poetry*, xxx.
221. Coffin, *Complete Poetry*, 371.

frequency of prayer and meditation in this, are often envenomed, and putrefied, and stray into a corrupt disease: . . . With the first of these I have often suspected my selfe to be overtaken; which is, with a desire of the next life: which though I know it is not meerly out of a wearinesse of this, because I had the same desires when I went with the tyde, and enjoyed fairer hopes than now: yet I doubt worldly encombrances have encreased it. I would not that death should take me asleep. I would not have him meerly seise me, and onely declare me to be dead, but win me, and overcome me. When I must shipwrack, I would do it in a Sea, where mine impotencie might have some excuse; not in a sullen weedy lake, where I could not have so much as exercise for my swimming. Therefore I would fain do something; but that I cannot tell what, is no wonder. For to chuse, is to do: but to be no part of any body, is to be nothing. At most, the greatest persons, are but great wens, and excrescences; men of wit and delightfull conversation, but as moales for ornament, except they be so incorporated into the body of the world, that they contribute something to the sustentation of the whole. This I made account that I begun early, when I understood the study of our laws: but was diverted by the worst voluptuousness, which is an Hydroptique immoderate desire of humane learning and languages: beautifull ornaments to great fortunes; but mine needed an occupation, and a course which I thought I entred well into, when I submitted my self to such a service, as I thought might imploy those poor advantages, which I had. And there I stumbled too, yet I would try again: for to this hour I am nothing, or so little, that I am scarce subject and argument good enough for one of mine own letters: yet I fear, that doth not ever proceed from a good root, that I am so well content to be lesse, that is dead.[222]

His apprehended lack of direction for his life is further expressed in the description that he gives of his life at Mitchem to Sir Henry Goodyer in 1608:

. . . And I which live in the Country without stupefying, am not in darknesse, but in shadow, which is not no light, but a pallid, waterish, and diluted one. As all shadows are of one colour, if you respect the body from which they are cast, (for our shadows upon clay will be dirty, and in a garden green, and flowery) so all retirings into a shadowy life are alike from all causes, and alike subject to the barbarousnesse and insipid dullnesse of the Country– onely the emploiments and that upon which you cast and bestow your pleasure, businesse, or books, gives it the tincture, and beauty.[223]

222. Coffin, *Complete Poetry*, 375–76.
223. Coffin, *Complete Poetry*, 379.

A Nocturnall Upon S. Lucies Day

'Tis the years midnight, and it is the days,
Lucies, who scarce seaven hours herself unmaskes,
    The Sunne is spent, and now his flasks
    Send forth light squibs, no constant rayes;
        The worlds whole sap is sunke:
The generall balme, th'hydroptique earth hath drunk,
Whither, as to the beds–feet, life is shrunke, –begot
    Dead and enterr'd; yet all these seeme to laugh,
    Compar'd with mee, who am their Epitaph.

Study me then, you who shall lovers bee
At the next world, that is, at the next Spring:
    For I am every dead thing,
    In whom love wrought new Alchimie.
        For his art did expresse
A quintessence even from nothingnesse,
From dull privations, and leane emptinesse:
    He ruin'd mee, and I am re–begot
    Of absence, darknesse, death; things which are not.

All others, from all things, draw all that's good,
Life, soule, forme, spirit, whence they being have;
    I, by loves limbecke, am the grave
    Of all, that's nothing. Oft a flood
        Have we two wept, and so
Drownd the whole world, us two; oft did we grow
To be two Chaosses, when we did show
    Care to ought else; and often absences
    Withdrew our soules, and made us carcasses.[224]

224. Grierson, *Metaphysical*, 13.

Sweetest Love, I Do Not Goe (Song)

Sweetest love, I do not goe,
For wearinesse of thee,
Nor in hope the world can show
A fitter Love for mee;
But since that I
Must dye at last, 'tis best,
To use my selfe in jest
Thus by fain'd deaths to dye;

Yesternight the Sunne went hence,
And yet is here to day,
He hath no desire nor sense,
Nor halfe so short a way:
Then feare not mee,
But beleeve that I shall make
Speedier journeyes, since I take
More wings and spurres than hee.

O how feeble is mans power,
That if good fortune fall,
Cannot adde another houre,
Nor a lost houre recall!
But come bad chance,
And wee joyne to'it our strength,
And wee teach it art and length,
It selfe o'r us to'advance.

When thou sigh'st, thou sigh'st not winde,
But sigh'st my soule away,
When thou weep'st, unkindly kinde,
My lifes blood doth decay.
It cannot bee
That thou lov'st mee, as thou say'st,
If in thine my life thou waste,
That art the best of mee.

Let not thy divining heart
Forethinke me any ill,
Destiny may take thy part,
And may thy feares fulfill;
But thinke that wee
Are but turn'd aside to sleepe;
They who one another keepe
Alive, ne'r parted bee.

—John Donne, 1612[225]

---

225. Coffin, *Complete Poetry*, 16.

A Valediction: Forbidding Mourning

As virtuous men passe mildly away,
And whisper to their soules, to goe,
Whilst some of their sad friends doe say,
The breath goes now, and some say, no:

So let us melt, and make no noise,
No teare-floods, nor sigh-tempests move,
T'were prophanation of our joyes
To tell the layetie our love.

Moving of th' earth brings harmes and feares,
Men reckon what it did and meant,
But trepidation of the spheares,
Though greater farre, is innocent.

Dull sublunary lovers love
(Whose soule is sense) cannot admit
Absence, because it doth remove
Those things which elemented it.

But we by a love so much refin'd.
That our selves know not what it is,
Inter-assured of the mind,
Care lesse, eyes, lips, and hands to misse.

Our two soules therefore, which are one,
Though I must goe, endure not yet
A breach, but an expansion,
Like gold to ayery thinnesse beate.

If they be two, they are two so
As stiffe twin compasses are two,
Thy soule, the fixt foot, makes no show
To move, but doth, if the'other doe.

And though it in the center sit,
Yet when the other far doth rome,
It leanes and hearkens after it,
And growes erect, as that comes home.

Such wilt thou be to mee, who must
Like th'other foot, obliquely runne;
Thy firmnes drawes my circle just,
And makes me end, where I begunne.[226]

---

226. Grierson, *Metaphysical*, 14.

These quotations seem to indicate that Donne was unhappy in the dependent situation that followed his marriage. The sense of direction and the hope in a promising future that had filled his life until that point was gone. Despite his numerous friends and his influential patrons, no new court appointment was forthcoming. He continued, however, to try to return to the same type of situation that he had held with Egerton. While thwarted in his career, he was faced with providing for his family as he waited for preferment, and his life became a series of short-term efforts, each begun with the hope of a new career and each ended with the frustration of unachieved ends.

One of the more promising of Donne's connections at this time was Sir Robert Drury. Donne made Drury's acquaintance in 1610, when he wrote a funeral elegy on the death of Elizabeth Drury, Sir Robert's fifteen-year-old daughter. This was followed by two long poems, the *Annivaersaries*, which commemorated the first and second anniversaries of her death. As a result of the ensuring friendship with Sir Robert and Lady Drury, Donne was invited to accompany them to Europe in 1612 and, upon his return, he and his family moved into a house on the Drury property in London, where they lived until he became Dean of St. Paul's. Although the association with Sir Robert yielded financial support for Donne and his family, it did not have the desired result of helping Donne to a court position. When Donne realized Drury's inability to aid his advancement, he turned for help to the Earl of Somerset, the king's current favorite. Somerset, Walton says, was optimistic that he could persuade James I to appoint Donne a Clerk of the Council. The King, however, refused the petition, replying: "I know Mr. Donne is a learned man, has the abilities of a learned Divine, and will prove a powerful preacher; and my desire is to prefer him that way, and in that way I will deny you nothing for him."[227]

---

227. Walton, *Lives of Donne and Herbert*, 24.

Goodfriday, 1613. Riding Westward

Let mans Soule be a Spheare, and then, in this,
The intelligence that moves, devotion is,
And as the other Spheares, by being growne
Subject to forraigne motions, lose their owne,
And being by others hurried every day,
Scarce in a yeare their naturall forme obey:
Pleasure or businesse, so, our Soules admit
For their first mover, and are whirld by it.
Hence is't, that I am carryed towards the West
This day, when my Soules forme bends toward the East.
There I should see a Sunne, by rising set,
And by that setting endlesse day beget;
But that Christ on this Crosse, did rise and fall,
Sinne had eternally benighted all.
Yet dare I'almost be glad, I do not see
That spectacle of too much weight for mee.
Who sees Gods face, that is selfe life, must dye;
What a death were it then to see God dye?
It made his owne Lieutenant Nature shrinke,
It made his footstoole crack, and the Sunne winke.
Could I behold those hands which span the Poles,
And tune all spheares at once peirc'd with those holes?
Could I behold that endlesse height which is
Zenith to us, and our Antipodes,
Humbled below us? or that blood which is
The seat of all our Soules, if not of his,
Made durt of dust, or that flesh which was worne
By God, for his apparell, rag'd, and torne?
If on these things I durst not looke, durst I
Upon his miserable mother cast mine eye,

Who was Gods partner here, and furnish'd thus
Halfe of that Sacrifice, which ransom'd us?
Though these things, as I ride, be from mine eye,
They' are present yet unto my memory,
For that looks towards them; and thou look'st towards mee,
O Saviour, as thou hang'st upon the tree;
I turne my backe to thee, but to receive
Corrections, till thy mercies bid thee leave.
O thinke mee worth thine anger, punish mee,
Burne off my rusts, and my deformity,
Restore thine Image, so much, by thy grace,
That thou may'st know mee, and I'll turne my face.

—JOHN DONNE, 1613[228]

228. Grierson, *Metaphysical*, 89.

Donne still resisted taking holy orders until 1615. During the time immediately before he was ordained, he evidently was still hoping that some civil post would be offered him. The record of these months which is revealed in Donne's letters indicates a quality of desperateness in his behavior. He stoops to levels of machination that he had not previously indulged in and his pleas for advancement reveal a loss of self-respect that would invite contempt, if the human misery that they reveal was not so strong. For example, his letter to Somerset in 1614: "I humbly therefore beg of your Lordship that after you shall have been pleased, to admit into your memorie, that I am now a year older, broken with some sickness, and in the same degree of honestie as I was, your Lordship will afford me one commandement, and bid me either hope for this business in your Lordship's hand, or else pursue my first purpose, [and] abandon all."[229]

When none of this desperate activity had the desired result, Donne finally succumbed and was ordained in 1615. Although he had protested on several occasions that he did not feel worthy to be ordained, his frenetic behavior before he took orders suggests that it was a desire for a secular career, rather than any feeling of unworthiness, that deterred Donne's entering the church earlier.[230]

Whatever hesitancy he had over this step prior to ordination seemed to disappear after he became a Deacon. He accepted his vocation with the same zeal that he displayed earlier in court life, and indeed, his skill as a courtier helped him as he sought preferment in the church. James, true to his promise, made Donne a court divine and made sure that he was given a doctor's degree from Cambridge in April, 1615. At first, Donne was given the living of Keyston, in Hunts.[231] Then, he became Rector of Sevenoaks in Kent. This was followed by an appointment as Reader in Divinity to the Benchers of Lincoln's Inn. Here, among his old friends, Donne preached scholarly sermons that would be appreciated by his educated audience.[232] He also preached before the king, adapting his language in these sermons to the idiom of the court.[233] It was while he was preaching at Lincoln's Inn that Ann Donne, his wife, died shortly after she had given birth to a still-born child. Of the twelve children she had had, seven were still alive and Donne assumed the full responsibility for them. He never remarried, and turned to his vocation with increased intensity.

229. Bald, *John Donne*, 291.
230. Bald, *John Donne*, 300–301.
231. Bald, *John Donne*, 539.
232. Bald, *John Donne*, 540.
233. Bald, *John Donne*, 540.

Since she whom I lov'd hath payd her last debt

Since she whom I lov'd hath payd her last debt
To Nature, and to hers, and my good is dead,
And her Soule early into heaven ravished,
Wholly on heavenly things my mind is sett.
Here the admyring her my mind did whett
To seeke thee God; so streames do shew their head;
But though I have found thee, and thou my thirst hast fed,
A holy thirsty dropsy melts mee yett.
But why should I beg more Love, when as thou
Dost wooe my soule for hers; offring all thine:
And dost not only feare least I allow
My Love to Saints and Angels things divine,
But in thy tender jealousy dost doubt
Least the World, Fleshe, yea Devill putt thee out.

—*HOLY SONNET XVII*, JOHN DONNE, 1617[234]

In 1621, Donne was named Dean of St. Paul's Cathedral. This post carried with it a generous stipend and the use of a large Deanery, into which Donne moved shortly after his appointment. The Deanship had both administrative and preaching duties. Donne himself now had the power of appointing aspiring clergy to various posts. He was responsible for overseeing the maintenance of the cathedral and for enforcing proper decorum within it. He was also responsible for preaching sermons at Paul's Cross. These sermons were lengthier than his Lincoln's Inn sermons and used a less academic vocabulary.[235] This was done, it is assumed, to assure the comprehension of the common people who gathered for these sermons. Although he was primarily known as a poet when he was given the Deanship, within a short time he built a reputation as a preacher that superseded his earlier fame and established him as a powerful orator.[236]

234. Coffin, *Complete Poetry*, 253.
235. Bald, *John Donne*, 539.
236. Bald, *John Donne*, 407–8.

> To John Donne
> Donne, *the delight of Phoebus, and each Muse,*
> *Who, to thy one, all other braines refuse;*
> *Whose every work, of thy most early wit,*
> *Came forth example, and remains so, yet:*
> *Longer a knowing, than most wits doe live;*
> *And which no'n affection praise enough can give!*
> *To it, thy language, letters, arts, best life,*
> *Which might with halfe mankind maintain a strife;*
> *All which I mean[t] to praise, and, yet, I would;*
> *But leave, because I cannot as I should!*
> —B[en] Jons[on] From Jonson's *Works, 1616*[237]

Izaak Walton describes Donne's preaching in his biography of Donne:

> Though much were expected from him, both by his Majesty and others, yet he was so happy—which few are—as to satisfy and exceed their expectations: preaching the Word so, as shewed his own heart was possessed with those very thoughts and joys that he laboured to distil into others: a preacher in earnest; weeping sometimes for his auditory, sometimes with them; always preaching to himself, like an angel from a cloud, but in none; carrying some, as St. Paul was, to Heaven in holy raptures, and enticing others by a sacred art and courtship to amend their lives: here picturing a Vice so as to make it ugly, even by those that practiced it; and a virtue so as to make it beloved, even by those that loved it not; and all this with a most particular grace and an unexpressible addition of comeliness.[238]

In 1623, Donne had been Dean for two years. Although he was still not fully recovered financially from his years of penury, the Deanship, and its attendant prebend, plus the rectories of Blunhan and Sevenoaks, gave him an income that promised to provide amply for his needs.[239] His preaching was recognized, he was in favor both at court, and in the ecclesiastical hierarchy. He could foresee rewarding work at St. Paul's and realistically hope for a Bishop's mantle. His life had finally, after years of frustration, assumed an order that he could appreciate and in which he could feel secure. It was at this time that he became ill with the fever that occasioned his *Devotions upon Emergent Occasions*.

---

237. Jonson, "Delight of Phoebus," 6.
238. Walton, *Lives of Donne and Herbert*, 27.
239. Bald, *John Donne*, 456.

No wonder his anger at the disruption of his life, no wonder his reiteration of the problem of change in a man's life! After years of attempting to achieve a secure position, what irony that that position be threatened by an illness of which he had no warning and over which he had no control. Thus, seen in the context of Donne's entire life, *Devotions upon Emergent Occasions* becomes more than the drama of what happens to a man when he is faced with life–endangering illness, more than meditations upon the significance of disease and suffering. It comes, indeed, at the climax of a life spent striving for the security of high office, for the accolades that come with recognized achievement, for the self–made order of hard–earned personal success. And because the things that Donne had worked for are ever present goals, translated here into a particular medium of expression, we too cry out with Donne "Variable, and therfore miserable condition of Man!"[240] as we experience the bottoming out that occurs when well made plans are interrupted by unknown variables, when expectations are shattered and the center goes awry.

In this larger context of bottoming out at a time when self–made success has come to be a reality, Expostulation XX may be seen to speak directly to that situation. In this Expostulation, Donne refers to the difference between God's order and personal ambition. "My *God*, my *God*, the *God* of *Order*, but yet not of *Ambition*, who assignest *place* to every one, but not *contention* for place, when shall it be thy pleasure to put an *end* to all these *quarrels*, for *spirituall precedences*?"[241] He then speaks of how attempts to order one's life outside of God's plan are doomed to failure: "As hee that would describe a *circle* in paper, if hee have brought that *circle* within one *inch* of *finishing*, yet if he remove his *compasse*, he cannot make it up a *perfit circle*, except he fall to worke againe, to finde out the same *center*, so, though setting that *foot* of my *compasse* upon *thee*, I have gone so farre, as to the *consideration* of my selfe, yet if I depart from *thee*, my *center*, all is unperfit. This proceeding to *action* therefore, is a returning to *thee*."[242] In the prayer that follows, Donne specifically enumerates the ways that he had used to protect his spiritual being against sin:

> I have, O *Lord*, a *River* in my *body*, but a *Sea* in my *soule*, and a *Sea* swoln into the depth of a *Deluge*, above the *Sea*. Thou hast raised up certaine *hils* in *me* heretofore, by which I might have stood safe, from these *inundations* of sin. Even our *Naturall faculties* are a *hill*; and might preserve us from *some sinne*.

---

240. Donne, *Devotions* (Sparrow), 1.
241. Donne, *Devotions* (Sparrow), 122.
242. Donne, *Devotions* (Sparrow), 123–24.

Education, study, observation, example, are *hills* too, and might preserve us from *some.* Thy *Church,* and thy *Word,* and thy *Sacraments,* and thine *Ordinances,* are *hills,* above these; thy *Spirit* of *remorse,* and *compunction,* and *repentance* for former *sin,* are *hills* too; and to the *top* of all these *hils,* thou hast brought mee heretofore; but this *Deluge,* this *inundation,* is got above all my *Hills*; and I have sinned and sinned, and multiplied *sinne* to *sinne,* after all these thy assistances against *sinne,* and where is there *water* enough to wash away this *Deluge*?[243]

243. Donne, *Devotions* (Sparrow), 125–26.

Satyre III

                    . . . On a huge hill,
Cragged, and steep, Truth stands, and hee that will
Reach her, about must, and about must goe;
And what the hills suddennes resists, winne so;
Yet strive so, that before age, deaths twilight,
Thy Soule rest, for none can worke in that night.
To will, implyes delay, therefore now doe:
Hard deeds, the bodies paines; hard knowledge too
The mindes indeavours reach, and mysteries
Are like the Sunne, dazling, yet plaine to all eyes.
Keepe the truth which thou hast found; men do not stand
In so ill case here, that God hath with his hand
Sign'd Kings' blanck-charters to kill whom they hate.
Nor are they Vicars, but hangmen to Fate.
Foole and wretch, wilt thou let thy Soule by tyed
To mans lawes, by which she shall not be tryed
At the last day? . . .
. . . That thou mayest rightly obey power, her bounds know;
Those past, her nature, and name is chang'd; to be
Then humble to her is idolatrie . . .
. . . So perish Soules, which more chuse mens unjust
Power from God claym'd, than God himselfe to trust.

                        —JOHN DONNE[244]

This detailed catalogue of defenses against spiritual sin can be transposed to show the ways that Donne sought to achieve protection against worldly failure. And his admission of his true helplessness against sin is analogous to his inability to ultimately protect himself against temporal misfortune. Thus, when he says in Expostulation XXI, "I have a *Bed* of *sinne*; *delight* in *sinne*, is a *Bed*; I have a *grave* of *sinne*; *senselessnesse* of *sinne* is a *grave*; and

244. Grierson, *Metaphysical*, 170–71.

where *Lazarus* had beene *foure daies*, I have beene *fifty yeeres*, in this *putrifaction*," he is speaking directly to his former inability to see God's order for his life.[245] "Why dost thou not call mee, as thou diddest him," he continues, "*with a loud voice*, since my *Soule* is as dead as his *Body* was? I need thy *thunder*, O my *God*; thy *musicke* will not serve me."[246] But he has already felt that thunder in the realization that his order is not God's order, and the subsequent healing that comes after violent disturbance, is even now being experienced by him:

> But O my *God*, my *God*, the *God* of all *flesh*, and of all *spirit* too, let me bee content with that in my *fainting spirit*, which thou declarest in this *decaied flesh*, that as this body is content to *sit still*, that it may learne to *stand*, and to learne by *standing* to *walke*, and by *walking* to *travell*, so my *soule*, by obeying this *thy voice* of *rising*, may by a farther and farther growth of thy *grace*, proceed so, and bee so established, as may remove all *suspitions*, all *jealousies* between *thee* and *mee*, and may *speake* and *heare* in such a *voice*, as that still I may bee acceptable *to thee*, and satisfied *from thee*.[247]

This nurturing and mutually shared growth is another dimension of security from that which was shaken by relapsing fever. In its wholeness of inclusion of God, it obliterates the old agony of the multifaceted Donne who yearned for union and yet held onto old behavior patterns. Donne further verbalizes in Prayer XXI his appreciation of his new state, in which surety is process, not specific goal; and salvation is both being and becoming, rather than defined end to be achieved:

> No more doe I, O *God*, now that by thy *first mercie*, I am able to *rise*, importune thee for present confirmation of *health*; nor now, that by thy *mercie*, I am brought to see, that thy *correction* hath wrought *medicinally* upon me, presume I upon that *spirituall strength* I have; but as I acknowledge, that my *bodily strength* is subject to every *puffe of wind*, so is my *spirituall strength* to every *blast of vanitie*. Keepe me therefore still, O my gracious *God*, in such a *proportion* of both *strengths*, as I may still have something to thanke thee for, which I *have* received, and still something to *pray for*, and aske at thy hand.[248]

---

245. Donne, *Devotions* (Sparrow), 129.
246. Donne, *Devotions* (Sparrow), 129.
247. Donne, *Devotions* (Sparrow), 131.
248. Donne, *Devotions* (Sparrow), 133.

Knowledge of Donne's lifelong struggle for the security of an appointment extends the understanding of the *Devotions upon Emergent Occasions*, placing them in the larger context of his total life experience. A knowledge of the events of his life also helps in understanding why Donne had such difficulty in relinquishing control over his life and why, after he achieved an empathic awareness of God and man, he continued his old close behavior in his convalescence.

The Donne that emerges from the biographical minutiae is a man who from early childhood experienced multiple levels of insecurity. Within his immediate family, he underwent the loss of his father when he was only four, and six months later he had to adjust to another different new family situation when his mother remarried. Three sisters had died before he went to college at age eleven and while he was a student at Lincoln's Inn his brother died after being imprisoned. Thus, by the time he was twenty, Donne had known the trauma of his father dying, his mother remarrying, three sisters dying of childhood diseases, and a brother dying as a result of religious persecution. If such a situation occurred today, one could easily predict the scars that Donne would carry into his adult life. Because death was a more common occurrence in the sixteenth century, we tend to minimize the amount of distress involved. Yet human nature is remarkably consistent, and it is predictable that Donne not only suffered at the time from these events, but that some of his adult behavior patterns stemmed from that early trauma.[249]

Linda J. Luecken in her major study of both psychological and physiological effects of parental death on young children observes that less research has been done on physiological effects than on psychological. However, there is a consistent appearance of anxiety and depression in later life if the child lacks a supportive environment at the time of the parent's death. There is, also, a clear relationship with physiological illness. Given the environment in which Donne was raised, with the fear of retaliation for not accepting the Church of England and his own family's suffering for choosing to remain Roman Catholic, it is no wonder he was anxious and depressed in later life and his health was compromised as an adult.[250]

If this postulation is applied to Donne, and his subsequent behavior is analyzed, his tendency to try to gain security through external ordering of and therefore control of his world seems to relate directly to the sense of confusion and disorder that he experienced when members of his family, especially his father, died.

249. Luecken, "Consequences," 397–416.
250. Luecken, "Consequences," 397–416.

A second large source of insecurity in Donne's formative years came from his family's adherence to the Roman Catholic religion during the reign of Elizabeth. The various forms of persecution that they experienced have been outlined earlier in this chapter. Physical danger, imprisonment, and even death were known within the immediate family. Exile, resulting in loss of English property, and financial depravation as a penalty for recusancy in England, also affected close family members. Donne, himself, did not receive a degree from Oxford because of scruples over the Oath of Allegiance.

In addition to overt repression by the established church and state, Donne grew up in an atmosphere alive with intrigue. His uncles were Jesuit priests, one of them sent to England as a missionary. Religious conviction involved his family in varying degrees of political activity. As he stated in the preface to *Biathanatos*, "I had my breeding and conversation with men of supressed and afflicted Religion, accustomed to the despite of death, and hungry of an imagin'd Martyrdome."[251] With the sense of superiority fostered by minority persecution came its corollary feeling of disassociation from the common Elizabethan culture. The swell of nationalism felt by Spenser and Shakespeare is not found in Donne. He remains, throughout his life, disassociated from communal response, always wary, always alert, always on guard. The survival techniques that the young Roman Catholic Jack Donne learned through his identification with a persecuted group continue to be used in later life. He guards his speech, is careful not to mention names and places in his letters, avoids direct political reference or opinion. An early witness to imprisonment and subsequent death as a result of minority religious involvement, he is prudent about controversial stands, careful to adhere to the court stance, politically vocal only along the approved court line. In those areas that he can identify as previously detrimental to his family, he is careful not to repeat or continue their behavior. And yet, beneath the caution of the third–generation Roman Catholic living in Anglican England, the behavior patterns of his family are played out in other parts of his life.

His parents' generation had not been content to conform openly and dissent in private, but instead drew the disapprobation of Queen and clergy by their open refusal to give up their beliefs and therefore lived out their lives under persecution. Donne created a similar environment of persecution for himself when he flaunted convention and married Ann More. Almost as if he could not stand the success for which he was destined as a member of the favored group of courtiers employed by Sir Thomas Egerton, the Lord Keeper of the Great Seal, Donne eloped with Egerton's niece, predicting

---

251. Coffin, *Complete Poetry*, 303.

quite accurately at the time that her angered father would proceed to ruin him by having him dismissed from Egerton's service. When the scenario was played out, Donne was back in the persecuted role in which he had been raised, and in which he functioned with ease. The subgroup of Roman Catholics who had made up his child's world was replaced by his close friends, who supported and succored him. He was deprived of his right to a court office, not for religious scruples but by the irrationality of Egerton's dismissal. Both deprivations seemed equally unjust and arbitrary. Having spent his inheritance, he was financially embarrassed and challenged to provide for an ever-increasing family in a hostile environment. And in his persistence in adhering to the unattainable goal of diplomatic position, he placed himself in an exile situation as effective as that which other members of his family had known for their religious beliefs.

Later, when he took holy orders and rose to success in the Church of England, this persecution behavior appears again, transposed into his perception of his relationship with God. This time he places himself in the minority by his insecurity over his salvation. He cannot accept the salvation so readily available to his listeners; apart, he agonizes over his soul. Eternal persecution is imminent in his sermons, the need to be right over points of belief and the subsequent dictates of behavior replay the old subgroup need for expertise once more. Caution over offending God follows earlier caution over language displayed as a courtier, and before that, as a Roman Catholic. Once again, early insecurity has dictated adult behavior that is repeated as a life script.

A third area in which Donne knew a lack of security was in his life at court. Life at the courts of Elizabeth, James I, and Charles I was subject to the pleasure and displeasure of the present monarch and his or her friends. As a young man, Donne saw his former commander, Essex, fall from favor, be sent to the Tower and executed. Sir Walter Raleigh also went that route, as did Northumberland, and the king's favorite, Rochester. Fortunes were made and lost through the cultivation of influential men, whose opinion could be changed by a well-placed piece of gossip as well as by overt behavior. Advancement, or lack of it, depended not on ability but on personality affinities. To remain at court successfully was to remain always on guard to possible threat, always cautious. The careful speech of a persecuted minority member fitted with the careful speech of the courtier. But at court, the enemy was not so readily defined as in the religious situation. One had few friends who could be trusted with candid opinion, few enemies so readily identified as such. Such a situation could be depended on to reinforce Donne's earlier feelings of wariness, and indeed, to initiate new low trust areas.

Finally, the natural world in which Donne lived also underscored the lack of security that men had while on earth. Plague was experienced several times during Donne's life, decimating the population, pointing out man's mutability. Infant mortality and death in childbirth were facts of life; war occurred intermittently throughout his life. Not only was life on this earth uncertain, but knowledge about the earth itself had undergone radical rethinking. The safe, predictable Ptolemaic universe of Aquinas and Dante had been destroyed by the discoveries of Copernicus and Galileo.[252] The Empyrean heaven and the four elements were no more, and Donne and his contemporaries were faced with a new world still largely understood in terms of an old philosophy and language. The excitement of discovery belonged to the previous age; the implications of that discovery to Donne's generation. Once again, in another area of life, he was faced with a set of data which could be predicted to stir up feelings of insecurity.

Thus, having experienced the insecurity of a broken home, a persecuted religion, court intrigue, pestilential illness, and geographical reorientation, it is not surprising that Donne learned survival techniques and continued to use this behavior after the initiating incident was over. Neither is it surprising that he searched for security not only through the use of these survival techniques, but also through the ordering of his own immediate environment which he felt he could control and which control made him feel secure. It is to be expected that the shattering of this imposed order would result in extreme anxiety. Finally, it is understandable why Donne continues to exhibit his old, close, non-trusting behavior even after he experiences the empathy that is possible through interdependent action and trust. Fifty years of programming cannot be so easily unlearned, and the incorporation of his new awareness will continue until his death. Although it is an experience different in kind from the bulk of his life, it, too, becomes part of the total experiential data that Donne uses to shape his philosophy.

---

252. Bronowski, "Starry Messenger," 189–218.

This is My Playes Last Scene

This is my playes last scene, here heavens appoint
My pilgrimages last mile; and my race
Idly, yet quickly runne, hath this last pace,
My spans last inch, my minutes latest point,
And gluttonous death, will instantly unjoynt
My body, and soule, and I shall sleepe a space,
But my'ever-waking part shall see that face,
Whose feare already shakes my every joynt:
Then, as my soule, to'heaven her first seate, takes flight,
And earth-borne body, in the earth shall dwell,
So, fall my sinnes, that all may have their right,
To where they are bred, and would presse me, to hell.
Impute me righteous, thus purg'd of evill,
For thus I leave the world, the flesh, the devill.

—HOLY SONNET VI, JOHN DONNE[253]

---

253. Grierson, *Metaphysical*, 86.

The ideas expressed in the *Devotions* appear in the sermons of the succeeding year. In the sermon preached at St. Paul's, on Easter Day in the evening of March 28, 1624, Donne vividly presents the problems that men face in trying to understand their behavior scientifically and contrasts this confusion with the immediate apprehension of the resurrected soul. The experiential problem is stated first:

> Here saies S. Augustine, when the soule considers the things of this world, Non veritate certior, sed consuetudine securior; She rests upon such things as she is not sure are true, but such as she sees, are ordinarily received and accepted for truth: so that the end of her knowledge is not Truth, but opinion, and the way, not Inquisition, but ease: But saies he, when she proceeds in this life, to search into heavenly things, Verberatur luce veritatis, The beames of that light are too strong for her, and they sink her, and cast her downe . . . and so she returnes to her owne darknesse, because she is most familiar, and best acquainted with it; Non electione, not because she loves ignorance, but because she is weary of the trouble of seeking out the truth, and so swallowes even any Religion to escape the paine of debating, and disputing; and in this lazinesse she sleeps out her lease, her terme of life, in this death, in this grave, in this body.[254]

This eloquent statement of man's inability to understand his life on his own and man's inability to maintain an inquiring and data-responsive attitude, is followed by a description of ultimacy apprehended: "But then in her Resurrection, her measure is enlarged, and filled at once; There she reads without spelling, and knows without thinking, and concludes without arguing; she is at the end of her race, without running; In her triumph, without fighting; in her Haven, without sayling: A free-man, without any prentiship; at full yeares, without any wardship; and a Doctor without any proceeding: She knows truly, and easily, and immediately, and entirely, and everlastingly."[255] It is the beatific vision of the XVIII prayer, painstakingly explained for the populace at Paul's Cross.

The ending of the sermon is Donne's statement of the distance between ultimate apprehension and its achievement in this world: "Surely the number of them, [souls] with whom we shall have communion in Heaven, is greater than ever lived at once upon the face of the earth: And of those who lived in our time how few did we know? and of those whom we did know, how few did we care much for? In Heaven we shall have Communion

---

254. Coffin, *Complete Poetry*, 399.
255. Coffin, *Complete Poetry*, 499–500.

of Joy and Glory with all, always... Where never any man shall come in that loves us not, nor go from us that does."[256] This ending is so personal. With it, Donne sums up the sources of his own suffering; of a life spent both in anticipating the behavior of those men who loved him not and suffering the grief of being separated from those whom he loved.

A second sermon at the end of 1624, again preached at St. Paul's on Christmas Day in the Evening, uses the example of a passing bell, to point out how God chooses to send his mercy:

> But we call not upon you from this Text, to consider Gods ordinary mercy, that which he exhibites to all in the ministry of his Church; nor his miraculous mercy, his extraordinary deliverances of States and Churches; but we call upon particular Consciences, by occasion of this Text, to call to minde Gods occasionall mercies to them; such mercies as a regenerate man will call mercies, though a naturall man would call them accidents, or occurrences, or contingencies; A man wakes at midnight full of unclean thoughts, and he heares a passing Bell; this is an occasional mercy, if he call that his own knell, and consider how unfit he was to be called out of the world then, how unready to receive that voice, 'Foole, this night they shall fetch away thy soule.'[257]

After various other examples of occasional mercies, Donne brings the sermon back to himself and his own illness: "If I should declare what God hath done (done occasionally) for my soule, where he instructed me for fear of falling, where he raised me when I was fallen, perchance you would rather fixe your thoughts upon my illnesse, and wonder at that, than at Gods goodnesse, and glorifie him in that; rather wonder at my sins, than at his mercies, rather consider how ill a man I was, than how good a God he is."[258] Thus, the experience described in the *Devotions upon Emergent Occasions* is becoming incorporated into Donne's totality of experience, and, incorporated, will influence the direction of his thought and understanding throughout the remaining six years of his life.

In those final years, Donne realized the stability of position and income that had been so elusive for the greater part of his life. His older children were grown, and he had the satisfaction of being able to provide for his mother in her old age. Records show that he helped his old friend, Sir Henry Goodyer, who had lost his fortune, and that his charities included helping debtors out of prison and providing for the sick. Thus, he reached out to

---

256. Coffin, *Complete Poetry*, 500.
257. Coffin, *Complete Poetry*, 500.
258. Coffin, *Complete Poetry*, 501.

others who were experiencing the two agonies of prison and sickness that were his personal fears. Whether his extended charities were merely a result of an increase in financial means, or whether they grew from the experience that he had had of being succored by an unknown parishioner's passing bell, is a matter of conjecture. Certainly, his behavior in those last six years displays a benevolence that is unrecorded prior to that time.

Bald points out that with advancing years, Donne knew the death of many of his old friends and was grieved by their loss. As his own life drew to a close, precipitated by an unidentified complaint, Donne made characteristically thorough preparations for his death. His estate was drawn up and his friends were called in and told goodbye. Two events, which reflect Donne's personality, are associated, as he intended they would be, with his death. The first event is the fact that, while alive, Donne commissioned Martin Droeshout to have an engraving done of himself in his shroud. He, himself, was the model for this unusual memorial and the etching reveals the gaunt, wasted appearance of advanced disease. After his death, this engraving was used as a model for an effigy by Nicholas Stone which was placed on his grave in St. Paul's. It is one of a few pieces to survive that church's destruction in the Great Fire of London in 1666.

Bald suggests that it is meant to be the resurrected Donne, who, facing east, is at last beholding God. His eyes are closed: "The sight and the Contemplation of God, and our present benefits by him, and future interest in him, must make us blind to the world so, as that we look upon no face, no pleasure, no knowledge, with such an Affection, such an Ambition, such a Devotion, as upon God, and the wayes to him . . . That powerful light felled Saul; but after he was fallen, his own sight was restored to him againe."[259] Perhaps Donne, resurrected, wished to be shown being filled with that light of God that no man can behold and not become blind.[260]

The statue, then, is an exceptionally appropriate memorial, combining the representational figure of Donne with religious symbolism, in a dramatic presentation typical of Donne's style. The second memorial that he left was his funeral sermon, delivered a few days prior to his death, entitled: "Death's Duell, or a Consolation to the Soule, Against the Dying Life, and the Living Death of the Body." In it, Donne takes the text: "And unto God (the Lord) belong the issues of death i.e. From death,"[261] and analyzes it as to how God will deliver us from death, how God will help us during death, and finally, as to how Jesus Christ delivered us by his death. It is a powerful

---

259. Coffin, *Complete Poetry*, 504.
260. Bald, *John* Donne, 536.
261. Coffin, *Complete Poetry*, 577.

sermon, different in tone from his Paul's Cross sermons, with a tight knit argument straight-forwardly developed. This is no longer Donne arguing with himself, but rather stating a credo he knows is soon to be experienced. In this sermon, the images of the passing bell and critical days appear briefly. In speaking of preparation for death, Donne states that it is not the moment of death but the entire life experience that must be evaluated. "Our criticall day is not the very day of our death, but the whole course of our life. I thank him that prays for me when the Bell tolles, but I thank him more that Catechises mee, or preaches to mee, or instructs mee how to live."[262] Thus even in his last days, the images formulated during his illness continue to be part of his vocabulary, harkening back to that earlier crisis in which he indeed faced death without the opportunity for extensive preparation. The sermon ends, characteristically, in a moment of drama. Donne invites the audience to share with him the passion of Christ, moving through the last hours of His life with Him, interpreting the actions, taking on himself the agony of his Lord until "hee gave up the Ghost; and as God breathed a soule into the first Adam, so this second Adam breathed his soule into God, into the hands of God."[263] With the completion of Christ's passion renewed in his mind, Donne had prepared himself for the order of his death, which was accomplished shortly thereafter on March 31, 1631. The need for intellectual understanding before integrated physical participation could be acquiesced to is evident in this work. Its achievement permits Donne's final sermon to attain the emotional closure that many of his other sermons lack.

Thus, a review of the major events of Donne's life places the *Devotions upon Emergent Occasions* in a perspective of total life experience that adds new insight into their meaning. The impact of sudden, life-threatening illness which struck when long-anticipated goals had just been achieved has been discussed as relevant in explaining the degree of upset that Donne verbalizes over his illness. Furthermore, a discussion of the various areas of stress that Donne had encountered throughout his life is helpful in understanding why Donne felt a need to control his life and why he continued to use controlling behavior after he had experienced that growth that comes through interdependency. In the discussion of these areas, it must be noted that the length and nature of this work has limited the extent to which various hypotheses have been developed. Pursuit of their implications are by design brief, although it is hoped that further work will be stimulated by their introduction here.

262. Coffin, *Complete Poetry*, 587.
263. Coffin, *Complete Poetry*, 593.

It is also recognized that all such hypotheses are by their very nature dependent upon some external structuring that must shape their conclusions. While it is the intention here to view Donne whole, and to comment on that totality, the limitations of individual interpretation, as well as personal bias, is fully recognized and reluctantly accepted. The final chapter is a discussion of the entire experience encountered in the *Devotions*, with specific emphasis on the objective and subjective apprehension of its significance.

Epilogue

The Experience: Objectively and Subjectively Perceived

No man is well, that understands not, that values not his being well; that hath not a cheerefulnesse, and a joy in it; and whosoever hath this *Joy,* hath a desire to communicate, to propagate that, which occasions his happinesse, and his *Joy,* to others; for every man loves witnesses of his happinesse; and the best witnesses, are experimentall witnesses; they who have tasted of that in themselves, which makes us happie.
MEDITATION VIII, *DEVOTIONS UPON EMERGENT OCCASIONS*[1]

---

1. Donne, *Devotions* (Sparrow), 43.

The preceding sections attempt to achieve a holistic understanding of John Donne's experience during his illness of 1623. Physiological aspects of the illness as described by Donne are presented in juxtaposition with a modern clinical textbook discussion of relapsing fever. Next, working away from the purely medical phenomena that both descriptions indicate, the emotional states experienced by Donne during this illness and convalescence are identified through a detailed analysis of the twenty-three Meditations. This analysis demonstrates that Donne experienced the following feeling states while ill: anger, loneliness, fear, depression, acceptance, and hope. It also reveals that although Donne presented a highly accurate account of his physical illness, his work is primarily concerned with presenting the effect of that illness in its totality on the man who was John Donne.

In order to understand more fully that experience, multiple methods of analysis have been used in the latter part of this book. Specifically, psychological, sociological, theological, and psychoanalytic approaches have yielded discrete insights into the source of Donne's emotional responses. For example, Donne's anger over his unexpected illness is first compared to the anger stage of terminally ill patients observed by Kübler-Ross.

Both Donne and these patients exhibit the rage of the innocent victim who has been singled out for misfortune without cause. He and they also express anger over their impotency to alter their condition. Secondly, his anger at having to stay in a bed and be dependent on others is shown to be related to that anger expressed by hospital patients who are called upon to adapt to the changed environment of the hospital and the changed behavior expected in the sick role. Furthermore, Donne's anger, when analyzed from a theological point of view, is seen to come from the frustration of his desire to order his own world, a desire that invites him to try to be God and is therefore doomed to failure. Also, in the religious sense, Donne is angry over not being able to understand why he, a good man, became ill. Finally, Donne's anger, when seen in the context of his life experience, is seen to stem from the frustration of having long worked for success thwarted by illness.

Thus, in order to understand the initial strong anger expressed by John Donne when he was stricken with relapsing fever, multi-level analysis is helpful. Each of the several methods gives valuable insight into the event. Each, however, while offering a way of structuring data so as to help comprehend what occurred, does not in itself satisfy the desire to understand the experience in its totality. Filtering—inherent in each process—narrows as it clarifies, simplifying the complexity of the behavior in order to explore fully specific sets of dynamics. And while a compilation of various analyses, such as this work offers, tends to restore these multiple levels of meaning inherent in the original response, through reworking the same data using methods derived from different disciplines, the impossibility of any ultimate statement becomes evident by the very nature of the method itself. Thus, this work offers the reader process rather than position, and invites participation in further redefinition.

At this point, the objectivity of interdisciplinary investigation evolves into the subjectivity with which each person understands the experience that was Donne's. Just as Donne's entire life shapes his sick–bed responses, each person's past affects the apprehension of that emotion. Each person's own experiences with stress, methods of coping, ability to respond empathically, and need to control are all brought to this account of illness and influence the perception of that event. The highly personal drama that unfolds in the *Devotions upon Emergent Occasions* thus results in an equally personal catharsis for those who read them today and will continue to redefine its meaning as it is incorporated into their lives.

> Our *criticall* day is not the *very day* of our *death*; but the whole course of our life. I thanke him that prayes for me when the *Bell* tolles, but I thank him much more that *Catechises*, mee, or preaches to mee, or *instructs me how to live*.
>
> —John Donne, *Death's Duel*, 1630[2]

---

2. Coffin, *Complete Poetry*, p. 587.

An Elegie Upon the Death of the Deane of Pauls, Dr. John Donne

Can we not force from a widdowed Poetry,
Now thou art dead (Great Donne) one Elegie
To crown thy Hearse? Why yet dare we not trust
Though with unkneaded dowe–bak't prose thy dust,
Such as the uncisor'd Churchman from the flower
Of fading Rhetorique, short liv'd as his houre,
Dry as the sand that measures it, should lay
Upon thy Ashes, on the funerall day?
Have we no voice, no tune? Did'st thou dispense
Through all our language, both the words and sense?
'Tis a sad truth; The pulpit may her plaine,
And sober Christian precepts still retaine,
Doctrines it may, and wholesome Uses frame,
Grave Homilies and Lectures, But the flame
Of thy brave Soule, that shot such heat and light,
As burnt our earth, and made our darknesse bright,
Committed holy Rapes upon our Will,
Did through the eye the melting heart distill:
And the deepe knowledge of darke truths so teach,
As sense might judge, what phansie could not reach;
Must be desir'd forever. So the fire,
That fills with spirit and heat the Delphique quire,
Which kindled first by thy Promethean breath,
Glow'd here a while, lies quench't now in thy death;
The Muses garden with Pedantique weedes
O'rspred, was purg'd by thee; the lazie seeds
Of servile imitation throwne away;
And fresh invention planted, Thou didst pay
The debts of our penurious bankrupt age;
Licentious thefts, that make poëtique rage

A Mimique fury, when our soules must bee
Possest, or with Anacreons Extasie,
Or Pindars, not their owne; the subtle cheat
Of slie Exchanges, and the jugling feat
Of two–edg'd words, or whatsoever wrong
By ours was done the Greeke or Latine tongue,
Thou hast redeem'd, and open'd Us a Mine
Of rich and pregnant phansie, drawne a line
Of masculine expression, which had good
Old Orpheus seene, Or all the ancient Brood
Our superstitious fooles admire, and hold
Their lead more precious, than thy burnish't Gold,
Thou hadst beene their Exchequer, and no more
They each in others dust, had rak'd for Ore.
Thou shalt yield no precedence, but of time,
And the blinde fate of language, whose tun'd chime
More charmes the outward sense; Yet thou maist claime
From so great disadvantage greater fame,
Since to the awe of thy imperious wit
Our stubborne language bends, made only fit
With her tough–thick–rib'd hoopes to gird about
Thy Giant phansie, which had prov'd too stout
For their soft melting Phrases. As in time
They had the start, so did they cull the prime
Buds of invention many a hundred yeare,
And left the rifled fields, besides the feare
To touch their Harvest, yet from those bare lands
Of what is purely thine, thy only hands
(And that thy smallest worke) have gleaned more
Than all those times, and tongues could reape before;
But thou art gone, and thy strict lawes will be
Too hard for Libertines in Poetrie.

They will repeale the goodly exil'd traine
Of gods and goddesses, which in thy just raigne
Were banish'd nobler Poems, now, with these
The silenc'd tales o'th'Metamorphoses
Shall stuffe their lines, and swell the windy Page,
Till Verse refin'd by thee, in this last Age,
Turne ballad rime, Or those old Idolls bee
Ador'd againe, with new apostasie;
Oh, pardon mee, that breake with untun'd verse
The reverend silence that attends thy herse,
Whose awfull solemne murmures were to thee
More than these faint lines, a loud Elegie,
That did proclaime in a dumbe eloquence
The death of all the Arts, whose influence
Growne feeble, in these panting numbers lies
Gasping short winded Accents, and so dies:
So doth the swiftly turning wheele not stand
In th'instant we withdraw the moving hand,
But some small time maintaine a faint weake course,
By virtue of the first impulsive force:
And so whil'st I cast on thy funerall pile
Thy crowne of Bayes, Oh, let it crack a while,
And spit disdaine, till the devouring flashes
Suck all the moysture up, then turne to ashes.
I will not draw the envy to engrosse
All thy perfections, or weepe all our losse;
Those are too numerous for an Elegie,
And this too great, to be express'd by mee.
Though every pen should share a distinct part,
Yet art thou Theme enough to tyre all Art;
Let others carve the rest, it shall suffice
I on thy Tombe this Epitaph incise.

Here lies a King, that rul'd as hee thought fit
The universall Monarchy of wit;
Here lie two Flamens, and both those, the best,
Apollo's first, at last, the true Gods Priest.
—Thomas Carew, 1633[3]

3. Grierson, *Metaphysical*, 177–80.

Appendix 1

Major Poems and Prose

		Page
Holy Sonnet I: *Thou hast made me, And shall thy worke decay?*	John Donne	1
Holy Sonnet X: *Death Be Not Proud*	John Donne	7
To a Lord, upon Presenting of Some of His Work to Him . . .	John Donne	39
Meditation XVII: *No man is an Iland* . . .	John Donne	47
Hymne to God My God, in My Sicknesse	John Donne	71
Holy Sonnet VII: *At the round earths imagin'd corners* . . .	John Donne	88
Book of Psalms: *Psalm 91*	King James Bible	92
The Canonization	John Donne	104
Holy Sonnet XIV: *Batter my Heart, three persone'd God* . . .	John Donne	104
A Hymn to God the Father	John Donne	107
Chaucer's Retractions	Geoffrey Chaucer	108
Divine Comedy, Paradise Canto XXXIII vv 123–145	Dante Alighieri	123
An Anatomie of the World	John Donne	127

Goe and Catch a Falling Star	John Donne	132
A Nocturnall Upon S. Lucies Day	John Donne	136
Sweetest love, I do not goe, for wearinesse of thee . . .	John Donne	137
A Valediction: Forbidding Mourning	John Donne	139
Goodfriday, 1613. Riding Westward.	John Donne	142
Holy Sonnet XVII: Since she whom I lov'd hath payd her last debt	John Donne	145
Donne, The Delight of Phoebus . . .	Ben Jonson	146
Satyre III: On a huge hill . . .	John Donne	149
Holy Sonnet VI: This is My Playes Last Scene	John Donne	155
Meditation VIII: No Man is Well . . .	John Donne	161
An Elegiie Upon the Death of the Deane of Pauls, Dr. John Donne	Thomas Carew	164

Appendix 2

Three Letters from John Donne

TO SIR GEORGE MORE

Sir,

 If a very respective feare of your displeasure, and a doubt that my Lord whom I know owt of your worthiness to love you much, would be so compassionate with you as to add his anger to yours, did not so much increase my sicknes as that I cannot stir, I had taken the boldnes to have donne the office of this letter by wayting upon you myself to have given you truthe and clearnes of this matter between your daughter and me, and to show you plainly the limits of our fault. by which I know your wisdom will proportion the punishment. So long since as her being at York House this had foundacion, and so much then of promise and contract built upon it withowt violence to conscience might not be shaken. At her lyeing in town this last Parliament, I found meanes to see her twice or thrice. We both knew the obligacions that lay upon us, and we adventured equally, and about three weeks before Christmas we married. And as at the doinge, there were not usd above fyve persons, of which I protest to you by my salvation, there was not one that had any dependence or relation to you, so in all the passage of it did I forbear to use any suche person, who by furtheringe of it might violate any trust or duty towards you. The reasons why I did not foreaquaint you with it (to deale with the same plainness that I have usd) were these. I knew my present estate lesse than fitt for her, I knew (yet I knew not why) that I stood not right in your opinion. I knew that to have given any intimacion of it had been to impossibilitate the whole matter. And then having these honest purposes in our harts, and those fetters in our consciences, me thinks we should be pardoned, if our fault be but this, that wee did not, by fore-revealinge of it, consent to our hindrance and torment. Sir, I acknowledge my fault to be so great, as I dare scarse offer any other prayer to you in mine own behalf than this, to beleeve this truthe, that I neyther had dishonest end nor meanes. But for her whom I tender much more than my fortunes or lyfe (els I would I might neyther joy in this lyfe, nor enjoy the next), I humbly beg of you that she may not to her danger feele the terror of your sodaine anger. I know this letter shall find you full of passion; but I know no passion can alter your reason and wisdome, to which I adventure to commend these particulars; that it is irremediably donne; that if you incense my Lord you destroy her and me; that it is easye to give us happiness, and that my endevors and industrie, if it please you to prosper them, may soone make me somewhat worthyer of her. If any take the advantage of your displeasure against me, and fill you with ill thoughts of me, my comfort is, that you know that fayth and thanks are due to them onely, that speak when theyr informacions might do good; which now it cannot work towards any party. For my excuse I can say nothing, except I knew what were sayd to you. Sir, I have truly told you this matter, and I humbly beseeche you so to deale in it as the persuasions of Nature, Reason, Wisdome, and Christianity shall inform you; and to accept the vowes of one whom you may now rayse or scatter, which are that as my love is directed unchangeably upon her, so all my labors shall concur to her contentment, and to show my humble obedience to your self.

    Yours in all duty and humbleness,
    J. Donne.

From my lodging by the Savoy,
2 Februa: 1601 [/2].
To the right wor. Sir George Moore, kt.
[Loseley MSS. —Kempe]

TO SIR GEORGE MORE

Sir, [Feb. 1601]

The inward accusacions in my conscience, that I have offended you beyond any ability of redeeming it by me, and the feeling of my Lord's heavy displeasure following it, forceth me to wright, though I know my faults make my letters very ungracious to you. Allmighty God, whom I call to witnesse that all my griefe is that I have in this manner offended you and him, direct you to beleeve that which owt of an humble and afflicted hart I now wright to you. And since we have no means to move God, when he will not hear our prayers, to hear them, but by prayeng, I humbly beseech you to allow by his gracious example, my penitence so good entertainment, as it may have a beeliefe and a pittie. Of nothinge in this one fault that I hear sayd to me, can I disculpe myselfe, but of the contemptuous and despightfull purpose towards you, which I hear is surmised against me. But for my dutifull regard to my late lady, for my religion, and for my lyfe, I refer my selfe to them that may have observed them. I humbly beseech you to take off these waytes, and to put my fault into the balance alone, as it was donne with out the addicon of these ill reports, and though then it wyll be too heavy for me, yett then it will less grieve you to pardon it. How little and how short the comfort and pleasure of destroyeng is, I know your wisdom and religion informs you. And though perchance you intend not utter destruction, yett the way through which I fall towards it is so headlong, that beeing thus pushed, I shall soone be at bottome, for it pleaseth God, from whom I acknowledge the punishment to be just, to accompany my other ills with so much sicknes as I have no refuge but that of mercy, which I beg of him, my Lord, and you, which I hope you will not repent to have afforded me, since all my endevors, and the whole course of my lyfe shal be bent, to make my selfe worthy of your favor and her love, whose peace of conscience and quiett I know must be much wounded and violenced if your displeasure sever us. I can present nothing to your thoughts which you knew not before, but my submission, my repentance, and my harty desire to do any thing satisfactory to your just displeasure. Of which I beseech you to make a charitable use and construction. From the Fleete 11 Febr. 1601.

Yours in all faythfull duty and obedience,
J. Donne

To the right wor. Sir Geo. More, kt.
[Loseley MSS.—Kempe]

TO SIR THOMAS EGERTON [1601]

The honorable favor that your Lordship hath afforded me, in allowinge me the liberty of mine own chamber, hath given me leave so much to respect and love myself, that now I can desire to be well. And therefore health, not pleasure (of which your Lordships displeasure hath dulld in me all tast and apprehension), I humbly beseeche your Lordship so much more to slacken my fetters, that as I ame by your Lordships favor mine own keeper, and surety, so I may be mine owne phisician and apothecary, which your Lordship shall worke, if you graunt me liberty to take the ayre about this towne. The whole world is a streight imprisonment to me, whilst I ame barrd your Lordships sight; but this favor may lengthen and better my lyfe, which I desire to preserve, onely in hope to redeeme by my sorrowe and desire to do your Lordship service, my offence past. Allmighty God dwell ever in your Lordships hart, and fill it with good desires, and graunt them.

Your Lordships poorest servant,
J. Donne

To the right honorable my very
good Lord and Master Sir Thomas
Egerton, knight, Lord Keeper of
The Great Seale of England.
[Loseley MSS.—Kempe][1]

---

1. Coffin, *Complete Poetry*, 380–383.

Appendix 3

John Donne's Mother, Elizabeth Heywood Donne

John Donne's mother, Elizabeth Heywood Donne, was a member of a noted intellectual family. Her grandmother, Elizabeth More, was the sister of Sir Thomas More who had been Lord Chancellor of England under Henry VIII. She married Judge John Rastell (1475–1536) who was a "lawyer of distinction and member of Parliament."[1] Their daughter, Joan Rastell, married John Heywood, an epigrammatist and writer of satire and interludes. Their daughter, Elizabeth Heywood, married John Donne. Their son was John Donne (1572–1631), poet and Dean of St. Paul's.[2]

"The Mores, Rastells, and Heywoods lived together in great harmony and in an intellectual comradeship which somewhat complicated the distribution of literary property. More was interested in drama and is traditionally reported to have had a hand in the production of interludes, as Rastell had; but Heywood, who from 1519 was employed at court as a musician, was the special playwright of the group and the most gifted of all interlude composers."[3]

All of these families were Roman Catholic. Sir Thomas More had been executed by Henry VIII for refusing to accept Henry's divorce from Catherine of Aragon. Donne's grandfather, John Heywood, a devout Roman Catholic, emigrated to Catholic Belgium early in Queen Elizabeth's reign to escape imprisonment. After Donne's father's death, his mother married Dr.

1. Baugh, *Literary History*, 358–61.
2. Walton, *Lives of Donne and Herbert*, 360–61.
3. Baugh, *Literary History*, 358–61.

John Syminges in 1588, President of the Royal College of Physicians, who, it assumed, was Roman Catholic. After Dr. Syminges's death, she married Richard Rainsford probably in 1590. Before September 10, 1595 they had gone abroad and subsequently lived in Antwerp.

Appendix 4

John Donne's Father, the elder John Donne, Ironmonger

John Donne's father, also named John Donne, was a wealthy merchant who, Izaak Walton says, was of Welsh descent.[1] In 1573, his father became Warden of the Worshipful Company of Ironmongers before his death in 1576.

The Worshipful Company of Ironmongers was incorporated under a Royal Charter in 1463. They were originally iron merchants. Today, the company is primarily a charitable institution. Ironmongers Hall is located in Aldersgate Street in the City of London. The original hall dating back to 1457 was on Fenchurch Street. It was rebuilt in 1587 and again in 1745. Finally, it was rebuilt once more after being destroyed on July 7, 1917 by a German bomb. The Ironmongers Company ranks tenth in the order of precedence of the City of London's twelve Livery Companies.

Livery Companies were of the nature of guilds. They dated from Saxon times and were usually of a religious kind. The societies would take care of their members when in need. They provided large charities for the poor of London. Charters were granted to them in return for large sums of money advanced to the national Exchequer by the Companies. Many of these Livery Companies possessed magnificent Halls.

Isaak Walton, who wrote the first biography of John Donne, although trained as a draper, joined the Ironmongers in 1618 and around this time he came to know John Donne.

---

1. Walton, *Lives of Donne and Herbert*, 5.

Appendix 5

Copernicus and Galileo Galilei

In 1543, Copernicus wrote *De Revolutionibus Orbium Coelestium*. This work put the sun at the center of the heavens. It upset ordinary persons who wanted earth in the middle as the Ptolemaic system had placed it.

In 1609, Galileo Galilei created the modern scientific method. At the age of 45, he developed the telescope. Henry Wotton—John Donne and Izaak Walton's friend who was the British Ambassador to the Doge's court in Venice—reported on the telescope and purchased one to send home to England. With it, four new planets and the moon could be seen.

What Galileo saw showed that the Ptolemaic heaven would not work. This discovery went against the belief of the Roman Catholic Church. The Counter Reformation had begun. In 1622, "Rome created the institution for the propagation of the faith." From it, we get the word "propaganda." Galileo's trial—found today in the Secret Archive of the Vatican Documents—started in 1611. The actual trial was in 1633.[2]

The 1616 Propositions to be forbidden were: 1. That the sun is immovable at the center of the heaven; and 2. "that the earth is not at the centre of the heaven, and is not immovable, but moves by a double motion."[3]

In 1624, Galileo wrote the *Dialogue of Great World Systems*. In 1632, he got it in print. In 1633, Galileo was summoned to Rome to appear before the Inquisition.

---

2. Bronowski, "Starry Messenger," 189–218.
3. Bronowski, "Starry Messenger," 207.

Author's Short Bio

Mary Ann Antley is a retired English professor who lives in Morganton, NC. She attends Grace Episcopal Church. A graduate of Agnes Scott College, she has an M.A. degree from Emory University. She recognized that the emotions that Kübler–Ross identified in her work with dying patients were also found in John Donne's *Devotions Upon Emergent Occasions*. The present book is the result of her insight and subsequent analysis.

Bibliography

Abrams, M. H., ed. *The Norton Anthology of English Literature*, vol. 1. 6th ed. New York: Norton, 1993.
———, ed. *The Norton Anthology of English Literature*, vol. 2. 1st ed. New York: Norton, 1962.
Alighieri, Dante. *The Divine Comedy of Dante Alighieri*. Translated by Charles Eliot Norton. 1891. Reprint, Cambridge, MA: Houghton Mifflin, 1941.
Allen, Don C. "John Donne's Knowledge of Renaissance Medicine." *Journal of English and Germanic Philology* 42.3 (1943) 322–42.
Andreasen, N. J. C. "Donne's *Devotions* and the Psychology of Assent." *Modern Philology* 62.3 (1965) 207–16.
Bald, R. C. *John Donne: A Life*. New York: Oxford University Press, 1970.
Baugh, Albert C., ed. *A Literary History of England*. New York: Appleton-Century Crofts, 1948.
Bennett, Joan. *Four Metaphysical Poets: Donne, Herbert, Vaughan, Crashaw*. New York: Vintage, 1960.
Bronowski, Jacob. "The Starry Messenger." In *The Ascent of Man*, 189–218. Boston: Little, Brown, 1973.
Buber, Martin. *The Prophetic Faith*. New York: Harper & Row, 1960.
Byock, Ira. Foreword to 50th anniversary edition of *On Death and Dying*, by Elisabeth Kübler-Ross. New York: Scribner, 2014.
Cecil, Russell L., and Robert F. Loeb, eds. "Relapsing Fever." In *A Textbook of Medicine*, 380–85. 9th ed. Philadelphia: Saunders, 1955.
Chaucer, Geoffrey. "Chaucer's Retractions." In *The Works of Geoffrey Chaucer*, edited by F. N. Robinson, 265. 2nd ed. Cambridge, MA: Riverside, 1957.
Churchill, Winston S. *The Island Race*. London: Corgi, 1968.
Coffin, Charles M., ed. *The Complete Poetry and Selected Prose of John Donne*. New York: Random House, 1952.
Coffin, Robert P. Tristram, and Alexander M. Witherspoon, eds. *Seventeenth Century Prose and Poetry*. New York: Harcourt Brace, 1946.
Donne, John. *Devotions upon Emergent Occasions*. Edited by Anthony Raspa. New York: Oxford University Press, 1987.
———. *Devotions upon Emergent Occasions*. Edited by John Sparrow. 1923. Reprint, Cambridge: University Press, 2013.
———. *Devotions upon Emergent Occasions Together with Death's Duel*. Ann Arbor: University of Michigan Press, 1959.

Fromm, Erich. *Escape from Freedom.* 1941. Reprint, New York: Avon, 1965.
Frye, Roland Mushat. *Shakespeare's Life and Times: A Pictorial Record.* Princeton: Princeton University Press, 1975.
Gardner, Helen, ed. *John Donne: The Divine Poems.* New York: Oxford University Press, 1952.
Goldberg, Jonathan. "The Understanding of Sickness in Donne's *Devotions*." *Renaissance Quarterly* 24.4 (1971) 507–17.
Gordis, Robert. *The Book of God and Man: A Study of Job.* Chicago: University of Chicago Press, 1965.
Gosse, Edmund. "John Donne." In *Encyclopaedia Britannica*, 8:417–19. 11th ed. 1910.
Grierson, Herbert J. C. *Metaphysical Lyrics and Poems of the Seventeenth Century: Donne to Butler.* 1921. Reprint, New York: Oxford University Press, 1959.
Hunt, Clay. *Donne's Poetry.* New Haven: Yale University Press, 1954.
Jonson, Ben. "Donne, the Delight of Phoebus." In *The Complete Poetry and Selected Prose of John Donne*, edited by Charles M. Coffin, 6. New York: Random House, 1952.
Kübler-Ross, Elisabeth. *On Death and Dying.* New York: Macmillan, 1972.
Luecken, Linda J. "Long-Term Consequences of Parental Death in Childhood: Psychological and Physiological Manifestations." In *Handbook of Bereavement Research and Practice: Advances in Theory and Intervention*, edited by Margaret Stroebe et al., 397–416. Washington, DC: American Psychological Association, 2008.
Martz, Louis L. *The Poetry of Meditation: A Study in English Language of the Seventeenth Century.* New Haven: Yale University Press, 1954.
Motion, Andrew. Preface to *Devotions upon Emergent Occasions and Death's Duel*, by John Donne. New York: Random House, 1999.
Nicolson, Adam. *God's Secretaries: The Making of the King James Bible.* New York: Harper Collins, 2003.
Papillon, Thomas. "Bell." In *Encyclopaedia Britannica*, 3:687–91. Rev. 11th ed. 1910.
Pepperdene, Margaret W., ed. *That Subtile Wreath: Lectures Presented at the Quatercentenary Celebration of the Birth of John Donne.* Atlanta: Darby, 1973.
Phillips, Charles. *The Illustrated Encyclopedia of Royal Britain.* New York: Metro, 2017.
Pinka, Patricia G. "John Donne." *Encyclopedia Britannica*, April 4, 2022. https://www.britannica.com/biography/John-Donne.
Raleigh, Walter, et al. *Shakespeare's England: An Account of the Life and Manners of His Age.* 2 vols. Oxford: Clarendon, 1916.
Saint Augustine. *The Confessions of Saint Augustine.* Translated by E. B. Pusey. New York: Dutton, 1907.
Shapiro, I.A. "Walton and the Occasion of Donne's *Devotions*." *Review of English Studies* 9.33 (1958) 18–22.
Smith, Emma. *The Making of Shakespeare's First Folio.* Oxford: Bodleian Library, 2015.
Tillich, Paul. *Dynamics of Faith.* New York: HarperCollins, 1958.
Toffler, Alvin. *Future Shock.* New York: Oxford University Press, 1971.
Trevelyan, G.M. *The Tudors and the Stuart Era.* Vol. 2 of *History of England*. New York: Doubleday, 1952.
Van Laan, Thomas F. "John Donne's *Devotions* and the Jesuit Spiritual Exercises." *Studies in Philology* 60.2 (1963) 191–202.
Varlow, Sally. *A Reader's Guide to Writers' Britain.* London: Prion, 1997.

Walton, Izaak. *Lives of Donne and Herbert*. Edited by S. C. Roberts. New York: Cambridge University Press, 1957.

———. *The Lives of Dr. John Donne, Sir Henry Wotton, Mr. Richard Hooker, Mr. George Herbert, and Dr. Robert Sanderson*. London: Society for Promoting Christian Knowledge, 1842.

White, Helen C., Ruth C. Wallerstein, and Ricardo Quintana. *Seventeenth Century Verse and Prose*. Vol. 1, *1600–1660*. New York: MacMillan, 1951.

Williams, Neville. *The Life and Times of Elizabeth I*. Edited by Antonia Fraser. New York: Shooting Star, 1995.

www.ingramcontent.com/pod-product-compliance
Lightning Source LLC
Chambersburg PA
CBHW051927160426
43198CB00012B/2069